RUMER GODDEN

by Hassell A. Simpson

s Series

Editor

VERSITY

Although Rumer Godden has published forty-one books in a writing career of nearly forty years, and although her works have been translated into a dozen foreign languages, and although they have always been admired by reviewers, so far she has been largely ignored by critics and academicians. To date only a handful of critical articles and chapters or sections in critical books have been devoted to Rumer Godden; and this study, the first full-scale analysis of her novels to appear anywhere, is an attempt to remedy that critical neglect. It is the first coherent treatment of all Miss Godden's fifteen novels, and it also considers many of her stories, poems, articles, and books for children as they relate to the novels. The study is justified today especially because she has published only one major novel in the past ten years and it must now be assumed that her work in the novel is nearly complete; although she continues to publish, other kinds of books are now her major interest. While this study is not a biography, it opens with a biographical chapter containing the most comprehensive account of Miss Godden's life that has yet appeared. The next chapter treats her first three novels in order, showing how she achieved in her third book mastery of her materials as well as public acclaim. Four chapters consider the novels under major thematic headings; and the last chapter analyzes the most recent novel as a culmination of the distinctive features of her style. Millions have warmed to the gentle irony and wit, the pure tones of English harmonized by a master arranger, and the delicate surprises Miss Godden has found in the most familiar situations. Her place in letters is already secure, as this book points out; if Rumer Godden is not yet among the most honored of English novelists, she has long since been among the most loved.

Godden

EAS

Rumer Godden

By HASSELL A. SIMPSON

Hampden-Sydney College

ABOUT THE AUTHOR

Hassell A. Simpson is professor of English, head of the Department of English, and chairman of the Division of Humanities at Hampden-Sydney College in Virginia. After graduation from Clemson University, he became an Army officer and later a newspaperman. In his native South Carolina he was columnist and correspondent for the *Anderson Independent* during college days, and later a copy-desk man and reporter for the *Greenville News*. Beginning a new career in academia, he took graduate degrees in English at the Florida State University, where he was for a time instructor in English. His master's and doctoral theses were critical studies of the works of William Faulkner. His articles and reviews have appeared in *Saturday Review, English Journal, Georgia Review,* and other periodicals. Before moving to Virginia, he taught for three years at Auburn University. He and his wife, who is an English teacher and poet, and their three sons live on the Hampden-Sydney campus.

York

44

To My Mother and the Memory of My Father

Preface

Rumer Godden's works have been published in a dozen languages, issued in hundreds of separate editions, and admired by reviewers and by readers in the millions. Forty-three books of hers appeared in the thirty-seven years from 1936 through 1972. These include fifteen novels, fifteen books for children, two collections of stories and verse, a narrative poem in one volume, a biography, a wartime service history, a reflective and autobiographical journal, two volumes of poems translated from the French, a reminiscence of their childhood written with a sister (Jon Godden, herself a noted novelist), an edition of verse by Emily Dickinson, another of Raphael's paintings illustrating the Bible, and even a book of recipes by Miss Godden's cook. There are also many uncollected poems, stories, and articles.

While the need for a full-scale study has been apparent for a number of years, so far the criticism of Rumer Godden as a novelist has been scattered: an article here, a chapter there, and of course hundreds of reviews of her books in periodicals. These pieces were naturally limited either to considerations of single books or to brief appreciations of a very general nature, and the latter are now outdated as Miss Godden has continued to publish. My study is an attempt to provide both a general estimate and a detailed analysis of her novels. What makes it unique is that for the first time it brings together treatments of all Miss Godden's fifteen novels, along with many of her short stories, articles, and books for children, as these are related to the novels in subject, theme, or style. The study is justified today as rarely before because she has published only one major novel in the past ten years; and, after a writing career of almost forty years, it must be assumed that her work in the novel is nearly completed.

The first chapter here is chiefly biographical; the second treats the first three novels in order, showing how, after two faltering starts, Miss Godden achieved in her third book mastery of her material and public acclaim; the next four chapters consider the novels under several major thematic headings; and the seventh chapter analyzes *In This House of Brede* as a culmination of the distinctive features of her style, summarizes significant criticism, and weighs the novels as contributions to English fiction. Although the thematic approach has entailed some scattering of remarks on individual books, it has seemed at last more sensible than the usual chronological arrangement, because Miss Godden's later novels are in many respects amplifications of themes outlined in her first three books. Nevertheless, the thematic approach has not precluded keeping in order certain important experiments in style, especially (in Chapter 4) the growth of her technical skill in representing several time levels and several viewpoints simultaneously.

Certain limitations should be clearly understood. Although comprehensive at the time of writing, this study cannot be definitive while Miss Godden is still working. It is not a biography; her early life, down through World War II, is reflected in work after work, and she has discussed her childhood in some detail and identified certain fictional incidents as autobiographical; nevertheless, she has been unwilling to allow much exploration of her private life since her first marriage, so I have refrained from speculating in print about parallels between her later life and her works. Finally, this book does not pretend to be more than a study of her novels; though her books for children are justly famed and frequently honored, and though the other works are thoroughly interesting in themselves, the demands of unity and the limitations of this series have excluded them except as they bear on their author as a novelist.

HASSELL A. SIMPSON

Hampden-Sydney College
Hampden-Sydney, Virginia

Acknowledgments

To these persons and institutions I should like to express my gratitude:

To Miss Godden herself, for patiently answering a number of questions, for correcting the chronology at an early stage, and for permission to quote from her several works.

To Dr. Walton R. Patrick of Auburn University and Dr. Sylvia E. Bowman of Indiana University; Mr. Ralph Thompson of the Book-of-the-Month Club, New York; Mr. Orville Prescott, formerly of the *New York Times;* Mrs. Annis Duff, formerly of The Viking Press, New York; Mr. Jean Renoir of Beverly Hills; and Dr. William C. Holbrook of Hampden-Sydney College, for help and advice.

To the President, the Trustees, and the Faculty Research Committee of Hampden-Sydney College, and to the Shell Companies Foundation, for assistance with the preparation of the manuscript.

And to the librarians and staffs of the Eggleston Library, Hampden-Sydney College; the Lancaster Library, Longwood College; and the Alderman Library, the University of Virginia.

I have also to thank the following for permission to quote from published material:

The Viking Press, Inc., for the works of Rumer Godden, and for the study of the Quin family tree from the endpapers of *China Court* by Rumer Godden, copyright © 1960, 1961 by Rumer Godden.

Harcourt, Brace and World, Inc., for the lines from *Four Quartets* by T. S. Eliot quoted in Chapter 4.

The Bobbs-Merrill Company, Inc., and Mr. Orville Prescott, for *In My Opinion: An Inquiry into the Contemporary Novel,* by Orville Prescott.

The National Council of Teachers of English and Professor William Y. Tindall, for "Rumer Godden, Public Symbolist," by W. Y. Tindall, from the *English Journal.*

The editors of the *Journal of English and Germanic Philology* and Professor John R. Frey, for "Past or Present Tense?" by John R. Frey.

Chronology

1907　Margaret Rumer Godden born December 10, Eastbourne, Sussex, daughter of Arthur Leigh Godden and Katherine Norah Hingley.

1908　June, taken by parents to India. Mr. Godden was in Indian navigation, and his family lived in several places on the rivers of Assam and Bengal.

1913　Sent to grandmother's London house for a year's stay; was returned to India in November, 1914, because of World War I.

1920–　Returned to England for schooling; attended five schools in
1925　five years, trained for ballet, and returned to India.

1928　Opened dancing school for children in Calcutta.

1934　Married Laurence Sinclair Foster at Calcutta. Father retired to first of two homes in Cornwall, Darrynane House.

1935　Completed *Chinese Puzzle*. Birth of first daughter, Jane.

1936　Publication of *Chinese Puzzle*. Gave up dancing school.

1937　January, *The Lady and the Unicorn*.

1938　Birth of second daughter, Paula, at parents' home in Cornwall.

1939　*Black Narcissus*, her first book to appear in the United States. Left Europe because of World War II, took daughters to India.

1940　*Gypsy, Gypsy*.

1941　September until March, 1942, residence at Jinglam on Namring Tea Estate in the Himalayas, as recounted in *Thus Far and No Further*.

1942　*Breakfast with the Nikolides*.

1944　*Rungli-Rungliot*.

1945　*Bengal Journey*, written for the Women's Voluntary Services (*A Story of the Part Played by Women in the Province, 1939–1945*). *A Fugue in Time* (in the United States, *Take Three Tenses*). Returned to England; lived in London.

1946　*The River* and *Thus Far and No Further* (American edition of *Rungli-Rungliot*).

1947　August 8, publication in United States of *A Candle for St. Jude* and her first juvenile book, *The Doll's House*. Moved to Arundel, Sussex.

1949　*In Noah's Ark* (verse). Moved to Speen, Aylesbury, Bucks; married James L. Haynes-Dixon in London; autumn, first visited America.

1950   *A Breath of Air.* Revisited India for filming of *The River* by Jean Renoir.

1953   *Kingfishers Catch Fire.* Moved to Whiteleaf, Princes Risborough, Bucks.

1955   *An Episode of Sparrows* and *Hans Christian Andersen* (biography).

1956   Moved to Highgate Village, London.

1957   *Mooltiki: Stories and Poems from India.*

1958   *The Greengage Summer.*

1960   Became a grandmother.

1961   *China Court.*

1962   Moved to Little Douce Grove, Northiam, East Sussex. *Prayers from the Ark,* translated from French.

1963   April, destruction by fire of Little Douce Grove; lived temporarily at Stubb Lodge, Brede, Sussex. October, *The Battle of the Villa Fiorita.*

1964   Revisited India. Returned to renovate Hartshorn House, a fifteenth-century dwelling, as new home at Rye, Sussex; lived meanwhile at Gun Garden, Rye.

1965   *The Creatures' Choir,* translated from French.

1966   *Two Under the Indian Sun,* with her sister Jon Godden.

1967   Visited the United States in connection with publication on December 1 of *The Kitchen Madonna,* a story for all ages.

1968   *Gone: A Thread of Stories* and *Mrs. Manders' Cook Book,* edited by Rumer Godden. Moved to Lamb House, Rye.

1969   Visited the United States, in connection with publication of *In This House of Brede,* first novel since 1963. *Operation Sippacik,* a book for older children; in London, *A Letter to the World,* by Emily Dickinson, edited by Rumer Godden.

1970   *The Raphael Bible,* the painter's works in the Vatican illustrating the biblical story.

1972   *The Diddakoi; Shiva's Pigeons: An Experience of India,* with text by Rumer and Jon Godden, accompanying photographs by Stella Snead.

Contents

Preface

Acknowledgments

Chronology

1. Two Brave Worlds: India and England   15

2. Where East Meets West   32

3. The Taming of Shrews   44

4. The River of Time   61

5. Children Adrift   80

6. Artifice and Romance   92

7. A Thinne Subtil Knittinge of Thinges   106

Appendices   133

Notes and References   136

Selected Bibliography   149

Index   157

CHAPTER 1

Two Brave Worlds: India and England

R UMER Godden's early life—spent partly in England, partly
in India—had a profound and pervasive influence upon her
literary work. That influence has grown more evident as her
career has advanced; for, over and over again, she has referred
in brief statements for publishers and the press to situations in
her life that have been mirrored in her work. But, because she
has carefully avoided public display of her personal affairs, the
organic relationship between fact and fiction was never so clear
as it has been since the publication of *Two Under the Indian Sun,*
(1966)[1] in which she and her older sister Jon Godden recall in
the most impressive detail a five-year period of their childhood
in the Bengal town of Narayangunj, eleven miles from Dacca.
The rest of Rumer Godden's life is less well known, but she has
spoken and written about it on many occasions, and some other
members of her family are well documented in print.

I *Her Family*

Margaret Rumer Godden was born at an uncle's house in
Eastbourne, Sussex,[2] on December 10, 1907, the second of four
daughters of a steamer agent, and was taken to India at the
age of six months.[3] Her father, Arthur Leigh Godden, had gone
to India at nineteen and had helped to clear and mark the
channels of the great Indian rivers for the shipping company
that employed him. He often said that he might have grown
rich had he chosen to settle in Calcutta, where the company's
headquarters were; instead, he preferred to be nearer the navi-
gational concerns of his business; therefore, he occupied mana-
gerial posts in a number of towns on the banks of the Ganges
and its network of branches.

Arthur's father had been a London stockbroker, and his maternal grandfather, Thomas Hewitt Key, was professor of comparative grammar at the University of London, an author, and a Fellow of the Royal Society. For a time Key was professor of mathematics at the then new University of Virginia. Miss Godden has remarked with pride that her great-grandfather[4] stayed in America only two years because he was unwilling to own slaves; presumably, he was also unwilling to live without servants. Incidentally, living and working abroad were nothing new in that family, for Professor Key's wife's brother, Albany Troward, who had fought at Waterloo, had died in India after long service there. Arthur Godden's mother's forebears were thus rather more distinguished than the Goddens themselves, who were "good yeoman stock . . . from Kent," as one of Rumer's maiden aunts once told her—or "pirates and smugglers," as another suggested darkly.

Rumer's mother, who had been Katherine Norah Hingley, came of a hard-working Quaker family whose members had created with their own hands positions of substance and influence for themselves through the manufacture of iron and steel in the North and Midlands of England. Rumer's great-grandfather Noah Hingley, like his father Isaac, began his career as an ironworker; but Noah had some share in the invention of the Nasmyth steam hammer that helped to modernize the industry, and was thereby enabled to leave riches to his large family. Curiously enough, although Rumer Godden's maternal ancestors were ironmasters, it is in her father's family that we find the name "Ironmonger"; her great-great-grandfather was Richard Ironmonger Troward—ironically, a solicitor. Miss Godden gave that name to two members of the fictional Dane family in *China Court*.

Noah Hingley's youngest son, Rumer's great-uncle, became Sir Benjamin Hingley, baronet, and served in Parliament for ten years. Family tradition had it that Sir Benjamin had intended leaving his wealth to his brother Samuel's children, including Rumer's mother, but that he died before his lawyer could arrive to write or change his will.[5] Nevertheless, Samuel Hingley's daughters appear to have been left in comfortable circumstances; for Katherine Norah lent money on several occasions to her husband, Arthur Godden, and her sister Mary had her own money and kept a horse when she lived with Arthur's family in India. By contrast, Arthur's mother and sisters, after his father had lost his money, lived in reduced circumstances when Arthur's children were young, as Jon and Rumer have indicated in *Two Under the Indian Sun;* however, in Rumer's short story, "Down Under the Thames," which in other respects appears to be a fictional rendering of her grandmother's household at the time of World War I, the family seems more substantial.[6] "We were not rich people but we must have had . . . eighteen servants then," Rumer has written elsewhere; still, despite "the semi-royal state in which the English lived in India, we were brought up quite frugally. . . ."[7]

Probably it has never been easy to rear children in India, but the difficulties for Europeans early in this century were such that, to parents nowadays, the thought of rearing four daughters under those difficulties is appalling. Yet Arthur Leigh and Katherine Norah Hingley Godden, at least as their daughters remember it, do not seem to have been often appalled. The ferocious climate, the rampant diseases, the political and religious friction among the native peoples and between them and the Europeans, the difficulty of obtaining clean food and water, and the scarcity of medical aid—all these factors stood in the way of parents' efforts to create a "European" setting for their children. But people do what they must; and, if the Goddens did not produce four proper little English schoolgirls, their daughters do seem to have achieved an effective balance between English and Indian cultures; for they accepted and learned from both environments.

II *Early Life*

Their first child, christened Ruth (better known today as Jon Godden), was born in 1906 at Midnapore in Bengal.[8] Sixteen months later the second daughter, Margaret Rumer Godden, was born in England; she was taken to India as an infant. The name Rumer, which has excited some curiosity among her readers, is a family name: the novelist's maternal grandmother was Harriet Rumer (Moore) Hingley, a lady of mysterious origins, who died on May 23, 1906,[9] a year and a half before the birth of Rumer Godden.

In 1913, when Rumer was five years old and Jon was six and a half, they were sent to their paternal grandmother's home, No. 4 Randolph Gardens, Maida Vale, London, while their mother and two younger sisters, Nancy and Rose, returned to India and their father. It was the custom, as the two elder daughters later wrote, for English parents in the East ("except those who were very poor or very wise") to have their children reared in England; and these two might have been separated from their parents for some years had it not been for World War I. For fear of the Zeppelin raids that did indeed kill or injure thousands in England, the two sisters were returned to India in November, 1914, after fourteen months in London.

The contrast between India and England could hardly have been greater; in tropical India, their household was relaxed, indulgent, swarming with servants and children of servants; but in chilly London, their grandmother's house was strict, severe, cramped by lack of money, and restricted by a formal piety. In England, they said their prayers aloud twice a day while their Aunt Evelyn Kate listened; and their lives "were lived a great deal round and in St. Augustine's," the High Anglican church standing opposite the house. Later, in Narayangunj with their parents, they did not go to church at all except at Christmas, when they attended Anglican services in a Masonic hall, and they said their prayers privately at bedtime. Despite the unevenness of their religious training, the sisters imbibed a sure sense of the Christian faith—mingled for a long time with their necessary knowledge of Hindu, Moslem, and Buddhist beliefs— and Rumer, in the intervals of wanting to become a writer, rather thought she might be a nun or a missionary[10]—ideals which, though unfulfilled, were perhaps omens of literary things to come.

But a writer she became and remained, except for a period of dancing and of teaching the dance. Her older sister Jon was a skilled painter who won a gold medal in a competition and later studied art; Nancy was a talented dancer as a child; and all the sisters except Rumer seemed gifted with good looks as well. Her portraits as an adult show a handsome, rather thin face with high cheekbones, firm lips, and faintly slanted and hooded eyes; but the child Rumer was conscious of being plain, of having, as the family said, "the Hingley nose," and of being a green-eyed child in a brown-eyed family; and so in defense she may have developed more fully than the others the literary talent that was evidently given to them all.

III *Childish Writing*

For all of them wrote stories, poems, and books that they painfully cut, stitched, and bound together and sometimes illustrated themselves. "Even at five I loved to write," Rumer has said, "and whenever opportunity offered would retire to the one private place in the house, the lavatory, where I would write hymns and odes, and at seven I completed my own life."[11] This "autobiography," as she has noted in *Two Under the Indian Sun,* was actually fictitious; it was drawn partly from a book she had read, and it contained this gem: "Peggy looked round and saw a tigiger and a loin roring at her." When Jon objected that there would have been no lion or tiger in a garden, "That doesn't matter," replied the youthful author. "This is writing." Nor has a little improbability ever seemed to trouble the author of such fictitious autobiography as, say, *Kingfishers Catch Fire,* the plot complications of which are resolved by a *deus ex machina.*

Like the little girl in *The River* who dreams in closely similar circumstances of becoming a great author, Rumer Godden wrote stories sometimes on her mother's note paper, and she had some published in Indian newspapers.[12] "None of these childish efforts," she once declared, "shows the faintest spark of originality or talent"[13]—a judgment that is probably far too harsh if the talents of Harriet in *The River* are at all comparable. (It is worth repeating here that the grandmother for whom Rumer Godden was named was *Harriet* Rumer.) Nevertheless, although the urge to be creative in words was strong in her, she experienced what many other writers have gone through: despite her sense of individuality and originality, she copied, and especially she copied poems: her verses were imitative of what she had read and loved. It was long before she could root out the traces of other artists in her own work, but that she did so alone and without assistance beyond the ordinary careless encouragement of family and friends is a source of justifiable pride. As she and Jon wrote, "One thing at least [Rumer] could claim: in writing she made her way herself."

IV *Joy and Fear*

Rumer Godden has sometimes called her childhood "halcyon" and "wonderfully happy."[14] So far as playtime is concerned, that must be very true. She and her sisters had each other as playmates; and for pets they had a mynah bird, rabbits, cats, dogs, guinea pigs, ponies, and a mongoose. There were also, less frequently, the servants' children as companions, and boys and girls from other European families who lived nearby. Moreover, apart from the colorful life of a polyglot Indian town, they traveled extensively, for in those days it was thought that Englishwomen could not bear the heat of summers in the plains and coasts of India. And so they went in the spring to "the Hills"—sometimes to the hills of Assam, or to Darjeeling under the snows of the highest Himalayan peaks, sometimes as far away as Kashmir, some seven hundred miles to the northwest—returning in early October. These were difficult and expensive journeys, often four or five days long; but they were considered worth the trouble and expense.

In these hill-country places of summer resort for Europeans, the Godden girls received their only formal schooling in India— in day schools rather casually run. They also had dancing lessons, for "Mam," as they called their mother, "was convinced, quite erroneously except for Nancy, that we could dance; we were convinced of it too and we danced anywhere and everywhere, at concerts and supper dances . . . [and] in hospital wards" since it was wartime. During one summer in the hills, Rumer learned painfully that Nancy was a better dancer than she. Again, in the painting competition in which Jon won her gold medal, Rumer experienced a crushing defeat when she overheard two ladies discussing her own contribution, "a study of a lotus flower floating on the water." Asked one lady, "What do you think it is?" The other answered, "A pink pig in blue mud."[15] In spite of such disappointments, Rumer later studied dancing and operated a dancing school; Jon, despite her gold medal for painting and her training in art, achieved fame not as a painter but as a writer.

At "home" (in the five years that Rumer lived with her family in Narayangunj), there was an equality among the sisters with only the slight difference of age to set them apart. The two older ones, when they returned from England, had lessons each day with their mother's sister, Aunt Mary, much as the sisters Bea and Harriet do in *The River*. Aunt Mary gave them piano lessons as well as arithmetic, spelling and grammar, literature, history, French, geography, and sewing. There had been brief experiments with governesses, but Jon's temper seemed ungovernable by them, and these ladies had soon departed. Later, in English schools, Jon and Rumer were to find that they could hold their own in Aunt Mary's subjects but that they had never been prepared in algebra, geometry, Latin, or science.

But the pleasure of play and the reassurance of discipline were by no means the full range of Rumer's early experience. Two rather cruel aspects of her life in India significantly colored her personality and, consequently, her work. On the one hand, there was the apparent cheapness of flesh in that land: the bodies of drowned animals were swept past on the river; the sweeper's old mother, caught up by a cyclone, was impaled on a bamboo pole (her demise is reflected in a nun's death in *Black Narcissus*); the sweeper himself killed his beautiful daughter out of jealousy when he found she had been living with the gatekeeper; and Rumer, having innocently placed two baby rabbits in the cage with a male rabbit, watched in horror as the buck tore the little ones to "bloody pulp." On the other hand, there was the awakening knowledge of evil within herself and those she loved: those baby rabbits she inadvertently destroyed had been jealously stolen by her from Nancy's cage; Rumer learned to lie when that course seemed easiest; and she received from Jon's lips the revelation that even parents are not to be trusted, for Jon knew that "Fa," their father, had shot their dog Sally because he could not bear her whimpering in pain during the night after her leg had been broken in an accident and set by a veterinarian. That incident was transmuted into fiction as the similar betrayal of Emily Pool, whose mother in *Breakfast with the Nikolides* hastily orders a veterinarian to put Emily's dog Don to death because of fear of its having rabies.

Indeed, the fear of rabies was all too familiar in Rumer Godden's experience. Her family had lived in Assam when there were only two daughters; three golden spaniels they had there developed rabies and were killed, but not before they had bitten everyone in the household. At that time "the only Pasteur Institute in India was in Kasauli, near Simla, five days' journey away." The journey had to be made, however, at enormous trouble and expense. Rumer did not remember, but Jon, who had been five, later recalled the injections—two in the stomach each day for two weeks—for every member of the family. The third daughter, Nancy, was born during this ordeal; and "it was no wonder," as Jon and Rumer wrote, that Nancy was "a small and sickly baby or that Mam was so ill she had to be sent back to England."[16] (The fourth daughter, Rose, was born in England in the following year, 1912.) Later, as if all Goddens were bound to suffer the same fate, Nancy herself was bitten by a dog someone brought to their house in Narayangunj; after it died of rabies, they all had to have the whole course of injections again. This time, however, a Welsh physician living in the town came to them.

Thus their fear of death could not entirely dispel danger by forearming them against it, for disease and danger were all about them. Every day, lacking refrigeration and a supply of pure water, "Mam" had to watch the milk and drinking water being boiled; every night mosquitoes had to be smoked out of the mosquito-netted beds, for malaria was frequent and quinine the only remedy; and "Mam" kept always near her a vial of anti-snakebite serum, for the bite of a cobra could kill in half an hour. A cobra eventually became the Serpent in the Garden of Rumer's beautiful fable, the little novel called *The River,* wherein the small son of a family closely resembling hers is bitten and dies and is buried the same day because in India such things have to be done quickly on account of the climate.

All of them worried about dying, but Rumer especially (like Harriet in *The River*) went through agonies of fear about death, not for herself, but for "the two props of her existence, Mam and Jon." No doubt that fear gave depth to the agonies of young Teresa in *Kingfishers Catch Fire* (Teresa's father has just died and her mother nearly dies of typhoid and pneumonia) and also to the Bullock children, likewise marooned in an alien land, in *The Greengage Summer*. Rumer's mother, however, provided some comfort—the sort of explanation of divine purpose of which Teresa's mother would be incapable: a baby, "Mam" said, cannot understand its parents' description of a projected journey, yet the journey is accomplished after all.

V   *Religious and Racial Influences in India*

Other religious influences were significant during Rumer's stay in Narayangunj. Hannah, the children's South Indian ayah, was a Roman Catholic Thomist whose devotion was strong and steady if somewhat simplistic; the cook was Catholic, too, but more leisurely in his observance. The table servants were Moslems, and the Hindus among the servants ranged from the Brahman gardeners to the untouchable sweepers. "Fa's" bearer was a Buddhist. The Hindu Feast of Lights, Diwali, was kept in the Godden home by Hindu, Christian, and Moslem alike; and they all joined in the observance of Christmas.[17] Whatever else such an environment might have produced, it helped young Rumer to develop a deep respect, not merely a tolerance, for the beliefs of others. When she taunted the head gardener by repeating the name of God, "Ram, Ram," Govind, deeply offended, took the unprecedented step of lodging a formal protest with her father, who reprimanded her sternly. The reprimand stung, and the memory lasted.

Hannah, the ayah, was quite different from her predecessors in the care of the Godden daughters. Gentle and loving, she managed to tame even the stormy Jon; her strength and tenderness are reflected in the ayah Nan in Rumer's novel *The River*. Before Hannah arrived, there had been a young Anglo-Indian nurse, Nana, who ruled the little girls secretly by her fierceness and by the fantastic tales she told of her romantic past. Nana, too, found her way into Rumer's fiction, as Annie (note the similarity of name), the Eurasian nursemaid of the short story "Tightrope."[18] Like the other Anglo-Indians (mixed bloods) of the Goddens' experience, Nana helped build in Rumer the mingled admiration, pity, and contempt that found expression most strikingly in her depiction of the Eurasian families of Lemarchant and deSouza in *The Lady and the Unicorn*. But Nana was not the only influence that helped Miss Godden write sympathetically of Eurasians, for in childhood Rumer herself felt the sting of contempt and the slap of pity from others after she returned to England in 1920 for her education. The halcyon days were over.

VI *Schooling in England*

"When I was twelve [Rumer Godden has written] my sisters
and I were sent home to school in England, where we were
quite unable to settle down and passed, in a stormy career,
from school to school, until finally we found peace and opportunity in Moira House in Sussex, which was run on free lines."[19]
Some of this difficulty is poignantly suggested in "The Little
Fishes," a *New Yorker* story that is part factual, part fictional,
for the two little schoolgirls are sisters named Ruth and Rumer
Godden; and they are thirteen and twelve years old, respec-
tively.[20] The two girls were not harmonious influences in the
Anglican convent school of St. Monica's. Sister Irene said, "What
queer little fishes!" Indeed, their accents, their sun-darkened
complexions, their names were very different from those of most
of their schoolmates, who were bound moreover by the sort
of "good sportsmanship" code that seems immutably British.
"Ruth and I were not sports," Rumer wrote, "and we were
telltales."

Despite their unhappiness, Rumer found some pleasure, when
she began to tell stories to another child, a half-wit. Others
heard them, and "soon I was being asked to tell them. . . .
It was so intoxicating to be suddenly interesting that success
went to my head." She began to tell lies and to cheat: "That
first school term was only eleven weeks long, but if it had been
eleven years Ruth and I could not have learned more of sadness
and duplicity."

In India a few months earlier, they had been secure, indulged:
"Our family were the most prominent Europeans there, and
our father, in his not very important position as manager of
a navigation company, ruled imperially." Now they were the
objects of wonder, pity, even contempt; they were miserably
unhappy, yet their condition might have improved had their
parents not intervened. Thinking that the strict religious observance of "St. Monica's school" was probably to blame for
her daughters' difficulties, their mother wrote to the superior
to ask that they be excused from attendance at services. "As
a matter of fact, the religion was one of the few things there
we really understood," Rumer wrote later. To the nuns, Mrs.
Godden's request was shocking; and not unnaturally they shut

out the young Goddens from the regular life in which the other girls participated. Rumer and Ruth, along with the half-wit and a little Chinese girl, were set apart. One day the sister superior, showing an old priest through the school, came upon the little band of misfits. "These," she said, "are the scum of the school." Ruth raised her hand and politely declined the epithet. Under the silent gaze of the old priest, Sister Laura Mary reddened and apologized: "I beg your pardon. I shouldn't have said that. No one is scum."[21]

On such meager assurances the fictional Godden sisters (but not their real counterparts) were able to survive. "The Little Fishes" contrasts two photographs taken a year apart at this period; the later one shows that the little misfits had become taller, heavier, more conventional schoolgirls: "Two little fishes, breathing naturally through our gills and swimming in the sea." But the real sisters, ill and miserably unhappy, were rescued by their mother. Nevertheless, like her earlier morbid fear of death, this situation no doubt contributed to the poignancy of Rumer Godden's many later stories dealing with children separated from parents in a strange land. Certainly her observation of the nuns left strong memories that stood the novelist in good stead when she came to write of the monastic life in *Black Narcissus* and *In This House of Brede,* and in an article about the "Heroic Monks of St. Bernard"; it also helped her to write *China Court,* structured on the hours of the religious day, and *St. Jerome and the Lion;* and it helped her to translate the poems of Carmen Bernos de Gasztold, who has lived for years in the Benedictine Abbey of Saint Louis du Temple in France. But for years afterward the experience of "St. Monica's" rankled with Rumer, and "The Little Fishes" was only one of several attempts to exorcise the memory of demonic nuns. In later life— after her conversion to Catholicism and after visiting in monasteries to prepare for the writing of *In This House of Brede*—she confessed that *Black Narcissus,* her first work treating convent life, was written "in a spirit of revenge" because the nuns had been "very cruel to my sister."[22]

Following this unsettling educational experience, Rumer Godden attended several schools until 1925; and, although she was unhappy in most of them, the schoolgirl continued to write. When she was about fifteen, she read an advertisement for a

vanity publisher; without telling her family precisely what she
was doing, she had a little booklet of verses printed. "They
were extremely bad," she has written, "and thank goodness not
a copy sold."[23]

VII   Career and Marriage in India

After her regular schooling, Miss Godden received training
in ballet at several schools in England, continuing an interest
that had begun in her childhood visits to the Indian hill stations.
In the dance, she says, she was "greatly influenced by Jaques-
Dalcroze."[24] In later years she was to write a novel (*A Candle
for St. Jude*) about a ballet company, its school and theater,
and its rather forbidding mistress; but she has said that
"Madame Holbein" reflects no particular teacher of her own.

She returned to India in 1925. In 1928, the year she turned
twenty-one, she herself, despite a lack of funds and over the
objections of her family, opened a dancing school in Calcutta,
the first of its kind in India. Her students numbered as many
as one hundred, and she was quite successful for about eight
years: "At one time I ran and owned a big dancing school in
Calcutta. Trained in London, I went out to make this school
the pioneer of its kind in India, for having written and produced
several ballets, I thought first to do this work seriously—instead
of writing."[25] After she had finished her second book, however,
she sold her school in order to spend more time writing.[26]

In 1934, she married a stockbroker, Laurence Sinclair Foster,
at Calcutta;[27] that was the year her father retired and went
to live in Cornwall.[28] She completed her first book, *Chinese
Puzzle*, writing in longhand, in 1935. Her first daughter, Jane,
was born that year, and in the same week the manuscript of
Chinese Puzzle was accepted; she says that she could not read
the proofs of the book, a circumstance which explains the strange
capitalization of nouns and adjectives.[29] The book was published
by Peter Davies in 1936.

A second daughter, Janaki Paula Mary, was born to Rumer
Godden Foster in 1938 at her parents' home in Cornwall;[30] and
in January of the following year she published her second novel,
The Lady and the Unicorn, written in intervals while working
at her dancing school.[31] She was still seeking a stance and a
style distinctively her own. *Chinese Puzzle*, though a charming

tale (rather, two charming tales), had been split by divergent themes and by a stylistic affectation; but *The Lady and the Unicorn* was incongruously both grim and lighthearted. She found her stance and style in *Black Narcissus*, which appeared in 1939; in this she drew a remarkable contrast between East and West, in the mission of a house of Anglican nuns living among natives of a radically different culture against a backdrop sketched from memories of visits to the Himalayas. A year later, Miss Godden took her readers to a European setting with *Gypsy, Gypsy*; that novel, too, featured an Englishwoman placed in violent contrast with the people of a foreign land and tongue, the French in this case. And, when France fell to the Germans during World War II, Rumer Godden herself was in Europe completing *Gypsy, Gypsy*. To avoid the dangers of war, she took her two daughters to India,[32] much as Louise Pool was to do in *Breakfast with the Nikolides* (1942); but this war, unlike that of 1914, seemed to be everywhere.

In July, 1941, "having lost everything we possessed in the retreat from Burma,"[33] she began the series of experiences recounted in *Thus Far and No Further*, a reflective and meditative work originally titled *Rungli-Rungliot*. During that month she traveled north from Calcutta to Namring Tea Estate (called "Rungolo" in the book) under the Himalayas, eighteen miles from Darjeeling, and chose as a residence a bungalow named Jhinglam ("Chinglam"). She moved into the house with her daughters and servants in early August and remained there until March, 1942. Although the war raged in other places, Jhinglam was an oasis of peace. In its solitude she found spiritual refreshment and time for her work, rising each morning at five-thirty to read and write.[34]

For three years, until 1945, she lived with her daughters in a small farmhouse high in the mountains of Kashmir,[35] a life reflected in that of the fictional Sophie Barrington Ward and her two children in *Kingfishers Catch Fire*. Rumer Godden has written:

Dilkusha, the house in *Kingfishers Catch Fire*, is a real house. I lived in it for several years. I left it reluctantly some time ago, but it is still there on the mountains above the lake.

The book is not an autobiography, but I lived in Kashmir much as my heroine, Sophie, did. Like Sophie, I made a herb farm, worked in my garden and taught my children.[36]

Another kind of book also grew out of Miss Godden's wartime years in India: *Bengal Journey* (1945), a history of the Women's Voluntary Service in Bengal. "During my last months in India in 1945 . . . I journeyed all over the Province of Bengal up to the then front line."[37] The resulting book describes and praises the selfless work of women as nurses, hostesses, and so on. *Take Three Tenses* was published, like *Bengal Journey,* in 1945. Called *A Fugue in Time* in England, this novel recounts in an original and very striking way a century in the life of a London house based, she says, on her Godden grandmother's home. In the same year, Miss Godden returned to England and lived in London.[38]

VIII   *Residence in England*

Rumer Godden's second marriage, to James L. Haynes-Dixon, a civil servant, took place in 1949; to him, she has dedicated *Hans Christian Andersen* (1959) and *In This House of Brede* (1969). She lived in several different houses in Buckinghamshire and at Highgate Village near London before renovating in 1961 Little Douce Grove at Northiam in East Sussex.[39] This house, curiously enough, had been the home of another prolific English Catholic woman novelist—Sheila Kaye-Smith, who wrote, among many others, two novels entitled *Joanna Godden* and *Joanna Godden Married.* Their heroine, a strong-willed, rather foolish woman like many of Rumer Godden's protagonists, lives in Sussex, too; "Joanna Godden's" family house, like many of Rumer Godden's fictional ones, is an active force in human life; and her farm is said to be just two miles from Rye, where Rumer Godden has settled most recently, and where Sheila Kaye-Smith also lived some years ago.

Little Douce Grove was a showplace upon which Mr. and Mrs. Haynes-Dixon lavished months of planning and supervision. An American visitor there has called it "one of the most beautiful dwelling places imaginable."[40] Unfortunately, Little Douce Grove was almost totally destroyed by fire in April, 1963, after they had lived there less than two years, and for a time the Haynes-Dixons occupied a succession of furnished houses.

Rumer Godden visited India again in 1964, having been there last in 1949 and 1950, for the filming of her book *The River*. She was busy during 1964 remodeling a fifteenth-century house at Rye in Sussex, which she and her husband occupied in the autumn. A few years later, at the invitation of the National Trust, they moved to Lamb House, Rye, formerly the home of Henry James.

Rumer Godden's two daughters by her first marriage are now grown, and there are several grandchildren. Throughout her long and productive writing career, Miss Godden has been busy with other concerns; but, despite them, she has been an active wife and mother. Not only have her books, both factual and fictional, testified to her love of houses and beautiful furnishings, of gardens and flowers, but she herself has repeatedly emphasized the fact—which only adds to the wonder that she should have found time (since 1945, the year when she returned to England) to publish nine novels and twenty-five other books in those twenty-seven years—not to mention the dozens of poems, essays, and stories, nor her many lectures and public readings. Moreover, as is already clear, she has not led the sort of settled existence that such productivity suggests; far from it. As she remarked with a trace of irony after the burning of her beloved Little Douce Grove, "I think the reason family houses are so important to me is that I have never had a settled home. Perhaps I am not meant to!"[41]

Nevertheless, the house of the title in *China Court* suggests the solid, comfortable kind of dwelling she loves; *Thus Far and No Further* shows to what lengths she has been willing to go in order to provide, even though imperfectly, the sort of house; and one inevitably recalls that the semiautobiographical Sophie of *Kingfishers Catch Fire* could not resist the trader "Profit David" when he offered a gorgeous rug or a lamp with a painted kingfisher. The novelist's sister Jon Godden Oakley has remarked that Rumer had in her English home "the same Persian carpet, or one exactly like it, that Sophie bought from her Profit David."[42] Again and again Rumer Godden has emphasized her love of having beautiful things about her. With some pain she noted in *Thus Far and No Further* a critic's charge that she was concerned with things, not people—a charge to which she was to give some credence a decade later by remarking, "I like a quiet family life and am passionately interested in houses, gardens, ballet, opera, theatre, herbs, and Pekinese—dispassionately interested in people."[43]

Since her return to England in 1945, she has become more and more occupied with writing for children. Her first juvenile book, *The Doll's House*, appeared in 1947; her second, *The Mousewife*, in 1951; and her third, *Impunity Jane*, in 1954. In the seventeen years from 1956 through 1972, twelve new juvenile books appeared. Her work in the novel, by contrast, seems to have slackened; in the same seventeen-year period, there were only four new novels from her pen. Oddly, the more recent novels have seemed less directly related to her own life than earlier ones had been. But Rumer Godden has been busy in other literary work; articles and essays appear several times a year, many of them dealing with writing, especially with writing for children. Her juvenile books have been well received. Reviewers generally have valued them for some of the virtues found in her novels—a lucid, graceful style; charm of subject; and a sense of warmth and immediacy.

Several of her works for children, notably *St. Jerome and the Lion*, are in verse; for poetry is also a continuing interest of Rumer Godden's. Not only does she publish verses from time to time, but she also writes and speaks about the art of poetry: "A love and understanding of poetry [Miss Godden once wrote] brings a perception, a sort of sixth sense, that makes its possessor quick to life—quick in the sense of being very much alive—quick to the world around him. It rescues him from dullness, gives him a sense of form, a mental discipline."[44] Parents, therefore, should encourage their offspring to read and enjoy poetry. It is never too early to begin, for false prejudices creep into adult estimates of poetry, fostered by popular misconceptions, by "memory exercises," or by bad teaching. In order to demonstrate her beliefs and to spread the delights of poetry among the young, Miss Godden for some years has taken "poetry tours, giving readings in libraries and schools." In one autumn, she has said, she "read poetry to more than 8,000 children of all ages and backgrounds";[45] and she has published in England several programs of poetry study for schoolchildren.[46]

In her person, as in her books, Miss Godden has a striking quality that has been reported time and time again by those who have met her: a strength often described as "steely" beneath a rather fragile appearance, a willed composure, and a driving determination.[47] Her older sister once put it this way: "She has a poet's detachment and spirit with an ability to work long and hard, although she is not strong and has endured many illnesses. A steely force and determination lie behind her small gentle appearance, green eyes and soft voice."[48] Phyllis McGinley wrote in 1961 of a meeting some years earlier:

there sat at tea with me that day this small, pretty, deceptively delicate-looking woman with prematurely gray hair and the gentlest of low voices. . . . Composure, I should say, is her chief attribute, a kind of willed serenity. . . . When, two years later, she came for a weekend to our Westchester suburban village it was a time of crises for me—a departing cook, a child ill with bronchitis, a dinner party only half arranged. She soothed the child, enchanted the company, made light of inconveniences even though at the time she herself was worn nearly to the breaking point. . . . It is this control of self and of her art which infuses her novels with such charm.[49]

The discipline to which Miss McGinley and other commentators pay tribute is the most impressive quality about Rumer Godden's books, although in making that statement one ought to specify that hers is a stylistic and linguistic discipline; for, in matters of probability and sentiment in fiction, she sometimes seems less controlled. Critics have sometimes complained that her stories seem fuzzy or sentimental, almost as if she were trying to make up for an imagined deficiency in passion about human beings by dwelling upon the thoughts and feelings of her characters and by choosing subjects that would appeal directly to the hearts of her readers. Certainly, in her first three books, she treated exotic subjects, sometimes whimsically, sometimes in fantasy, and in the process she matured as an artist. For her, discipline has not meant abstaining from romance.

CHAPTER 2

Where East Meets West

A S a child Rumer Godden had found that "writing" need not conform to the immutable laws of the real world. Her delight in the power of literary creation, discovered thus early and unchecked by the advice of more mature writers, led not only to the juvenile gaucheries mentioned in the preceding chapter but also to the innocent crudities of her first two published books, written when she had long since left childhood behind. That she moved swiftly through these two books and almost immediately into the writing of an international best seller of far greater substance and skill is testimony that in the four-year span between 1936 and 1939 Rumer Godden "made her way herself" to artistic maturity. In the process, she became more and more aware of her power and of her rightful province. That province was the little-known land where East meets West, where mind and imagination intersect, where body and soul dwell briefly together. To that province, she brought not a profound mind or an articulated philosophical world view but a sensitive awareness of beauty, a feeling heart, and an experience of both joy and pain that embraced half the globe. She also brought to her task a powerful determination to master her materials and her craft.

I Chinese Puzzle

Her very first book, *Chinese Puzzle* (1936), was a rather whimsical production founded on the situation of an ancient Chinese gentleman's being reincarnated as a Pekingese dog in present-day England. The dog himself is the author of this double autobiography; he holds the pen in his mouth to write, and he names a spaniel as his literary executor.[1] As if these were not sufficient departures from conventional fiction practice, Miss

Godden capitalized all nouns and their modifiers, and occasionally other words as well; this habit gives a curious appearance to the printed page, as in the following passage that describes the gentleman's first awareness of his new canine condition:

> I am Old Man, I am Young Dog—Here I was rudely interrupted by my Legs. I, Advocate of Stately Movement and Dignified Behaviour, Observer of Ceremonies and Correct Demeanour, could not control my Legs.
> They were golden, they gambolled. I carried a Flower in my Mouth.[2]

This stylistic trick may be justified in several ways. For instance, the capitals do convey a sense of dignity—somewhat irrelevant, perhaps, as in the quoted passage, and yet quite apt precisely because the irrelevant dignity of the printed words parallels the irrelevant dignity of a gentleman-become-dog. Or, one might say, the capitalization gives a feeling of antiquity, or of a foreign idiom, recalling the early days of European printing—though that alone can hardly suggest Chinese antiquity or strangeness. But Miss Godden does not attempt to justify that style for these or any other reasons; on the contrary, she has stated that she wrote the book in longhand, that she had no opportunity to see the proofs, and that she was horrified at the results in print which seemed to her "extraordinarily affected."[3]

Although she regretted having employed the capitals, in some other respects Miss Godden anticipated her critics and disarmed them in advance. There is, for instance, a striking passage in which Ting-Ling, the Pekingese and former man, explains to his disciple, the cocker spaniel Truthful James, what he has written:

> As my Disciple he was daily growing more intelligent, more grave and thoughtful; the others said he was growing old. He was becoming a Good Critic.
> "The First Part of your Book," he said once, "is all about People, the Last Part all about Dogs. Isn't that a little peculiar?"
> "I can't help it," I answered. "In my First Life I knew only People, now I only know Dogs. I have to write what I know."[4]

Not only does this passage tend to forestall unfavorable criticism of the two-part nature of the book, but is also answers in advance

those who would quibble with Miss Godden's use of both
English and Chinese or, say, Indian characters and backgrounds,
as well as those who might find it odd that she herself should
write most frequently about women, children, houses, and
furnishings.

In other respects, however, *Chinese Puzzle* is open to criticism.
Any reader may wonder why, of all possible pairs of incarna-
tions, the author chose a modern dog and an ancient man; it
is no satisfactory answer to say that the man was Chinese and
that the dog's Pekingese ancestors were, too. No doubt one
answer lies in Miss Godden's loving conception of the Pekingese
as a wise little creature, manlike in some attributes.[5] Even so,
the viewpoints were not aptly chosen, for neither the Chinese
man of old nor the modern Pekingese dog expresses Miss Godden's feelings on this subject. The dog comes closer than the
man, indeed, to such an expression, for Ting-Ling compares
his canine acquaintances with human beings from his former
incarnation. Furthermore, he speculates upon the nature of dog
and God, creates his divinity in his own image (noting that
God spelled backward is Dog), and looks forward to a time
when a Dog-Messiah will come to place dogs on an equal level
with men and free them from the worship of man. On the other
hand, the Chinese gentleman, Wong-Li, makes no comment on
the nature of dogs; and, although his first-person narrative is
charming and almost whimsical in tone, it has nothing whatever
to do with Pekingese. It does have to do with his deep love
for his cousin and bride in his former life, the Lady Little Finger.

A second answer to the question of why Miss Godden chose
the man-dog pair lies in the title, *Chinese Puzzle;* it refers to
the Peke's puzzlement at being sent back to life in a second
birth as a dog, not a man. His "Chinese puzzle" is solved in
an epilogue after he has written his own two-life story: childless
in his first incarnation, he has returned to life in order to fill
the "Hole" left by his departure. Seeing the five dog puppies
he has fathered, in an excess of joy he rushes outside—and
under the wheels of an automobile. That is to say, Ting-Ling
dies fulfilled at last; as Wong-Li, he had died unfulfilled. Now
the Lady Little Finger and her loving husband may be reunited
for eternity.

It is scarcely necessary to suggest the influence of Eastern mysticism on Rumer Godden's conception of this story. *Chinese Puzzle* was followed by *The Lady and the Unicorn* (1938), which, like the first book, contains two parallel stories. An unsatisfactory novel in several respects, it realistically indicates that the destinies of persons are only partly in their control. In it, as in *Black Narcissus,* flesh and spirit have very little connection.

II The Lady and the Unicorn

The surface story is that of the Lemarchants, a half-caste family, nominally English, who live their precarious lives in a grimy quarter of Calcutta, that capital of perpetual human misery. Father is a shiftless European ne'er-do-well; Mother, now dead, was an Asian; Aunt Anna is a widow, shortsighted and helpless to direct the family. The seventeen-year-old twins, Belle and Rosa, embody the racial and cultural contrasts within their family. Belle is loose of speech, of conduct, and of attachment to her relatives; Rosa is admirable in the main, but she is driven to and fro by poverty, shame, and the warmth of her feelings first for Robert deSouza, the landlord's gentle son, and then for Stephen Bright, an authentic English gentleman and not-quite-true heart. The younger daughter, Blanche, who is in everyone's way, finds only temporary affection in briefly possessing a goldfish.

The parallel story, so different in tone and content as to be a disruptive force, deals with former inhabitants of the deSouza house in which the Lemarchants and several other families presently live. Boy, the ancient houseman, tells Blanche that the old structure is haunted; sometimes a ghostly carriage and horses are seen leaving at night and galloping through the closed front gates. Stephen, persuading Rosa to a belief in the possibility of ghosts, says that, to an observer "up above, they are seen all in one, past present and future co-existent"—a theme to which the author returns again and again.[6] Sure enough, Robert and Rosa, Blanche, Aunt, and Mr. Mascarenes (another tenant), all see a pretty lady resembling Rosa, or a little white dog called Echo, or both; and sometimes they hear the clatter of horses' hooves and the rumble of a carriage. Gradually, they discover that the old house has a romantic past that is represented by the pretty lady and her dog and by a wall relief of the dog (revealed when some plaster falls), a sundial discovered in the front garden, and the figure of a unicorn molded in the plaster over each window in a wing of the house.

Meanwhile, the story of the living persons grows more and more hopeless and painful. The twins lose their virtue to upper-class Englishmen, Blanche nearly dies of acute amoebic disentery, the house is torn down to make way for a cinema palace. And, as the present-day story becomes more painful, the ghost story becomes more romantic, as if Rumer Godden and her characters were retreating from reality into fantasy. Yet the wild romance of the ghost story comes to nothing—is shattered by grim realities. Rosa and Stephen, seeking knowledge of the former inhabitants of the house, have pondered the sundial, for they are intuitively certain that it contains the solution to the mystery; but only after the house is torn down does little Blanche, secretly poking through the ruins, find that the dial itself has come apart and that glittering stones—diamonds?—were hidden in the joint. Ironically, she is too young, too naïve, and too fearful to suspect the value of her discovery or even to report it; therefore, the grand coincidence, carefully fore-shadowed and developed, does nothing more than add one more bitter irony to a story already ironical. All in all, *The Lady and the Unicorn* represents an arbitrary smashing of pretty or innocent things. Miss Godden was approaching unconsciously the theme she was to display at length in *The River* and (with her sister) in *Two Under the Indian Sun*—the cheapness and the transitory nature of life.

This unhappy portrayal of Eurasians in *The Lady and the Unicorn,* especially in its suggestion that the girls are victimized by well-to-do Englishmen, probably led to the novel's being banned in certain clubs in Calcutta.[7] Rumer Godden had learned from her English school days that unthinking prejudice can leave permanent scars; and her Eurasians, neither easterners nor entirely westerners, were particularly suited to dramatize the clash of alien cultures.

A much later story called "Tightrope" (published in 1953)[8] shows that the novelist did not easily put such concerns behind her. Three little English sisters live in a provincial Bengali town, as the four little Goddens did. The nursemaid Annie is a Eurasian (like Nan in *The River* and the Goddens' real-life nana).

She is also an orphan, or so the mother tells the little girls; but Annie herself claims that she, the daughter of an Italian count, was kidnapped, brought to India, and reared by nuns. She has, she says, a talisman on a cord around her neck, "the fingernail of St. Teresa encased in solid gold," given her by the Pope as a "royal" child. Although Annie is a very bad nurse for children, the little girls themselves behave very well for her; they were formerly so bad that previous nurses had left the family. The tale suggests that the transparent magic of Annie's lies is the very food that the imagination of children feeds upon. Not only is she secretly of the nobility, she says, but she is also related to a wonderful circus troupe, the Four Delaneys.

When the Four Delaneys come to town, the children's father suggests that Annie take the girls to see the show. Annie resists but finally relents, and the reason for the resistance is immediately plain to the reader though not perceived by the children. The circus is a pathetic entertainment composed entirely of the Four Delaneys and their assorted talents. Little Tybalt, the tap dancer, is neat, sweet, perfect—but Mama is fat; Irma, old and stringy; and Clifford fumbles his magic tricks. After one miserable act, the distinct sound of a slap is heard offstage, and Clifford shouts at the audience, "Go home!" Outside after the show, the young narrator sees Annie offering money to her cousin Irma. "Behind me, through the shutters, came the gay light sound of Tybalt's tap-dancing. It was my dream come true. He was dancing on a tightrope that was broken."[9] The daydream of royalty and grand entertainment has become the narrator's nightmare. Annie has moved on a tightrope as precarious as the existence of her cousins, and their balancing acts reflect the tenuous position not only of Eurasians in India but of the poor everywhere.

Having exorcised in *The Lady and the Unicorn* the sting of her exclusion from the society of her first English school, Rumer Godden was ready to attack the tormentors themselves—the nuns who had once excluded her and Jon. It would be years, however, before readers in general would understand the nature of the attack or even perceive that one had been made; and even then Rumer had to tell them about it in an obscure note in a publishing-trade journal, for the new book was so delicately wrought that to casual eyes it seemed quite harmless.

III   Black Narcissus

Rumer Godden's third novel was her first to be published
in the United States. *Black Narcissus* arrived in July, 1939, and
some reviewers were ready to dismiss it hastily as light summer
fiction.[10] But, as the season passed, it became evident that American readers had discovered a refreshingly new novelist.[11] That
Miss Godden had already published two novels in England was
scarcely known here; for that matter, a wide knowledge of *Chinese Puzzle* and *The Lady and the Unicorn* would not have
enhanced her reputation. As it was, the grace of her style in
Black Narcissus, the charm of the Himalayan background, and
the pungency of her subtle humor were presently acknowledged;
and the novel had twelve printings in its first three months.
Apparently, no one perceived the personal bitterness the narrative embodied.

Very little happens—on the surface—in *Black Narcissus.* Such
plot as it has, however, is drawn with clarity and precision;
and it is played out like a three-act drama. The first act opens
as five sisters of the Anglican Order of the Servants of Mary
pause for tea during their journey on horseback to the General's
Palace at Mopu, where they intend to establish a school and
hospital. Complications are provided for the first and second
acts by the world, the flesh, and—who knows?—perhaps the
Devil as well, in the persons of the practical Mr. Dean, the
General's agent; Dilip, the perfumed youth who is the General's
nephew and the new school's most difficult student; Kanchi,
the ripe orphan girl; and the sisters themselves, who are as
oddly assorted and ill prepared for their new work as it would
seem possible to be. At the third-act curtain, all the threads
are drawn up again as the sisters break another horseback journey at the same spot—and this time they drink their tea in
the knowledge that they will never return to Mopu.

It is not giving away any secrets to expose their failure; indeed, it is clear today, as it was not when the book appeared,
that Rumer Godden meant the sisters to fail; and that one purpose of her writing was to strike at the nuns who had mistreated
her and her older sister and who had failed to understand the
little Anglo-Indians and to appreciate their worth, as Chapter
1 of this study has explained. Thus, from the very first page

of the novel, an aura of failure hangs over the Convent of St. Faith, for it is not the first religious foundation in the General's Palace. One year earlier the Brothers of Saint Peter established there "Saint Saviours's School," but it had only two students, and the brothers themselves remained only five months.

The General's Palace itself is one reason for these failures. The General's father had built the house for his women; it was a one-story affair, a "palace" only by courtesy. Its history, known to the native servants and by them made known to the sisters, could not fail to strike such persons as wildly inappropriate—as if a convent were to be established in a former brothel. Another cause of the failure is the character of the natives whom the school and hospital are to serve. Their traditions contain nothing that would invite either modern healing or Christian teaching, and they come only because the General has given orders and money to insure their attendance. It is not explained why the sisters thought it necessary to establish a foundation at Mopu; presumably it was sufficient for them that the General gave the house and wished the people to have learning and medicine.

Still another reason for the failure of the mission is to be found in the character of the sisters themselves, surely the unlikeliest missionary sisterhood anywhere. The Superior is the youngest of the five: Sister Clodagh, an Irish aristocrat, took holy orders because her intended husband went to America to make his fortune without her. She is brisk, efficient, and intelligent, but she is not very patient or religious or even compassionate. Clearly she is not the person to make a success of an enterprise like theirs, though she might well have succeeded at many other tasks. Sister Briony, the oldest nun, is the housekeeper, plain and practical, who is always worrying about her keys and her cupboards. Sister Blanche is plump, pretty, sentimental; she has been called "Sister Honey" since her school days. Sister Phillippa, the gardener, is shy and quiet, and the first to break under the strain of life in the Palace. But the most difficult of all is Sister Ruth, nervous and intent, clever and proud; she chafes under discipline and restraint, and her discontent seems to focus at last in a passionate desire for Mr. Dean, the Englishman who is the General's resident agent.

Dean is yet another reason for their failure, quite apart from his necessary presence as manager and as a man. Unlike the sisters, he is irreligious, practical, compromising, masculine. Unlike them, he has come to an understanding with his environment. But the most powerful reason for the failure of the convent is the pervasive presence of the Himalayan snows. The Palace—now the Convent—is on a ledge in a hill facing, across the river valley, the mountain Kanchenjungha. The eye is drawn unwillingly to the peaks of the range where ice winds constantly blow; and the sisters, especially Clodagh, find that even their devotions are colored by their consciousness of the eternal snows. Their religious observances in this setting seem trivial and incomplete, the more so by contrast with the perpetual meditation of a holy man called the Sunnyasi, who sits motionless in all weathers under a deodar tree, head shaved, arms and chest bare to the winds, looking out toward the snows. The sisters are impressed by the Sunnyasi:

"I think there are only two ways to live in this place," said Sister Phillippa: "you must either live like Mr. Dean or like the Sunnyasi; either ignore it completely or give yourself up to it."

"Which is which?" asked Sister Clodagh, and she added, "Neither would do for us."[12]

Although the forces allied against the sisters are very powerful, they mercifully are not allowed to perceive them all at once. Their difficulties arise one by one. The house needs repairs—and only Mr. Dean, skeptical and plain-spoken, can properly supervise the workmen; meanwhile, he distracts the sisters with his whistling and his mere masculine presence. One day Dean brings a voluptuous girl, Kanchi, to the sisters to be educated and, he says, cloistered for a while. She is an orphan and has no prospects for marriage, and she is far too pretty to be left to her own devices. Then the General's nephew and heir, the young General Dilip Rai, comes to be educated; and somehow he cannot be turned away either, although he is too old, too male, and too exotic by far. He even wears perfume, a scent called "Black Narcissus"; so Sister Ruth calls him Black Narcissus "because he's so vain."[13] Thus the title of the novel functions on several levels. The scent itself, and on a man, is very exotic; and the dark young man himself, though harmless, is extremely self-centered, even narcissistic. The youth and his scent, like the Sunnyasi and the snows, are beyond the comprehension of these nuns and are therefore very dangerous to them. He soon proves how dangerous by seducing Kanchi, thereby reaffirming the original purpose of the Palace as seraglio. (Further comment on this symbolic title may be found in Chapter 7.)

Not only in the school but also in the hospital the sisters fail to establish and maintain an effective ministry to the people. Mr. Dean has warned them that they must never touch hopeless cases, for the natives would blame the treatment for the eventual death. Nevertheless, Sister Honey secretly treats a baby with a fatal illness; when the baby dies, the secret medication is brought to light, and the people, who are furious, say that Sister Honey killed him. Sister Ruth cracks under the strain of the tension that follows, and finally she runs away from the convent to throw herself at Mr. Dean. He sends her away; but, when she does not appear at the convent, the night is spent in searching for her. Next morning, as Clodagh is about to ring the convent bell, she is attacked by Ruth in a suspenseful struggle at the railings high above sharp spikes of cut bamboo below the house; the maddened nun, falling upon them, is fatally impaled.

The scandal of Sister Ruth is the end of the order's usefulness at Mopu, and the sisters are recalled. But all has not been entirely in vain. Clodagh receives from their Mother Provincial a message that astonishes her: "This is the first letter I have ever had from you that pleased me in spite of the terrible news it brought. In it I seem to find a new Clodagh, one whom I had long prayed to meet."[14] Clodagh has grown in wisdom, in humility, and perhaps in love. The others do not seem to have gained, however; and all the death and disappointment are high prices to pay for Clodagh's late maturation. Nevertheless, the bitterness of this unsatisfactory conclusion has the tang of real experience, and it no doubt brought the author some relief from her resentment against the Anglican nuns of her school days.

At this point, it may be well to emphasize Rumer Godden's unflinchingly realistic view of experience. Her situations are sometimes farfetched, her characters are occasionally one-dimensional, but the plot resolutions in her novels are never entirely happy endings. Life itself does not pinch off consciousness at crucial moments when everything seems to be going swimmingly, and neither do her stories. Instead, the lives of men and women run on steadily ("Time Is a Stream" is the name of a short story of hers) and, for the most part, imperfectly. In *Black Narcissus* one finds for the first time in Rumer Godden's work a unified, fully articulated plot; a balanced, full-circle structure; motivated characters who grow through experience; and a consistent attempt to mirror reality—in a setting of great beauty and fascination. It is, in short, a solid, workmanlike novel.

Unlike her nuns, Rumer Godden had found her vocation and her place, and it was not entirely her fault that she was admired for some of the wrong reasons. What appealed to readers in 1939 as a softly sweet story of love and a tenderly sad tale of religious devotion foiled by the crass concerns of this world turns out to have been a personal revenge, well disguised as a sensitive novel. Small wonder that, as has already been stated, the motion-picture version drew down the wrath of Catholics who failed to recognize the nuns as Anglican;[15] though the Catholics were mistaken in that one detail, they were not mistaken as to the story's unflattering depiction of the religious life. It would be fourteen years before a short story called "No Virtuoso" would treat with sympathy the devotion of a girl taking the veil, and thirty years before another novel of Rumer Godden's, *In This House of Brede,* would present the religious life fairly as one that might be chosen, not selfishly as shelter from the world or as a second choice for a jilted girl, but selflessly as a glory to God.

IV   Early Tendencies

The three novels published in the 1930's seem at first to have little in common. *Chinese Puzzle* suggests that the need of living creatures to reproduce their kind may require reincarnation, even in another shape, for those who fail at procreation in one lifetime (not incidentally, it was completed during the author's first confinement); and it finds godlike qualities in both men and dogs. *The Lady and the Unicorn* presents the seamiest side of life for Europeans in India; it suggests that half-caste persons, especially girls, during the British rule had little hope of a comfortable or secure existence, and that the ghosts of a romantic past are all around, especially in old houses. And *Black Narcissus* reached beyond fantasy to find in the Himalayan mountains a spiritual power that seemed to the Anglican nuns to dwarf both them and their faith.

In tone and attitude, as well as in theme, the three books are different. *Chinese Puzzle* is light, tender, delicate—and at times unpleasantly cute. *The Lady and the Unicorn* is alternately grim and fantastic and is ultimately unconvincing: the heroine deliberately gives her body to the young English gentleman she loves and then persuades the son of her Portuguese landlord to marry her and legitimize the other man's child. But in *Black Narcissus* Miss Godden found a greater unity of theme and style; the contrast between East and West—which she had attempted in *Chinese Puzzle* and had established well in *The Lady and the Unicorn,* and to which she would return in many later works—found its most powerful expression in the nuns' vain struggle against the terrain, the customs, and the spiritual attitudes of the East. Moreover, the delicacy and the precision of her language lent themselves well to descriptions of the Palace and the mountains, to wry and witty speeches, and even to the violence of Sister Ruth's death.

Yet the first three novels had certain common attributes, notably their striking contrasts between East and West and between sensuality and spirituality. The three books also delimited the fields which Miss Godden would cultivate throughout her career as a writer. *Chinese Puzzle* introduced her readers to these subjects and attitudes: the charm of the East, a love of dogs, especially Pekingese, and the biology of reproduction. *The Lady and the Unicorn* added these: the gap between parent and child, the passion and vulnerability of the female adolescent, the pathos of neglected children, effeminacy in boys and men, the endless fascination of old houses, and the lives of the English in India. *Black Narcissus* continued the study of contrasts between easterners and westerners, and the interest in adolescent passion and in charming old houses. It added gardens, mysticism, and (in Sister Clodagh) the strong-willed sort of woman represented in the central figures of several later novels.

CHAPTER 3

The Taming of Shrews

A T the heart of Rumer Godden's novels and stories is a rigorous concept of the household sanctified by marriage as the central fact of creative human experience. Lacking such a household, a woman must seem less than womanly. Sister Clodagh of *Black Narcissus* was a forerunner for several of the later fictional women without men—women who, by the exercise of masculine strength of will, very nearly dominate all those around them. Although she failed at last to establish her order's hospital and school in the shadow of the Himalayas, Clodagh always moved in an aura of command, and she strongly resented encroachments upon her authority. Like the Sister Superior, several other determined single women willfully tread on the sensitivities of other persons in order to pursue their own aims: Aunt Barbe of *Gypsy, Gypsy,* Selina Dane of *Take Three Tenses,* and Madame Holbein and Hilda French of *A Candle for St. Jude.*

I Women Without Men

These single women are shown to be foolish or incomplete in one way or another, and in that respect they resemble two married characters separated from their husbands, Mrs. Grey of *The Greengage Summer* and Fanny Clavering of *The Battle of the Villa Fiorita.* Flying in the face of convention, the two married women outwit themselves and bring unhappiness on others. Two other wives (Louise Pool of *Breakfast with the Nikolides* and Sophie Barrington Ward of *Kingfishers Catch Fire*), like all these women, defy the authority of men before being brought to their senses.

Of these willful women, the most forceful and least believable is Madame Barbe de Longuemare of *Gypsy, Gypsy* (1940), an Englishwoman who married the master of the Château de St. Lieux in Normandy. Her husband has been dead for some months when Barbe decides to leave Paris and return with her niece Henrietta to the Château. Perpetually discontented, Barbe is represented as cold, cruel, and selfish. Her niece fears and even hates her, and with good cause, for Barbe envies the girl her youth and resilience. Indeed, she envies all freshness and innocence, for she longs to refresh her jaded mind and body; and she feels that she can best refresh herself by corrupting the person or the soul of an innocent. One reason for this belief is that she has heard of an Oriental legend that intercourse with a virgin child can cure venereal disease.

A spiritual corruption seems to be her object, and she chooses her victim carefully: a Gypsy camping on her land. Gradually, by alternately severe and indulgent treatment of the young man and later of his children as well, she takes from him his wildness, his freedom, his independence of movement and feeling, and makes him her dependent. But this loss of freedom is not the greatest one the Gypsy suffers; he and his children are gradually corrupted by unearned gifts. Barbe's fickle generosity teaches the Gypsies to whine, to covet, to beg—and to steal. The Gypsy's wife succeeds in persuading her husband to leave the estate and Barbe's influence, but he cannot bring himself to leave without asking for the money Barbe has promised him for the purchase of a horse, and he visits her at night to make the request. When Henrietta and Barbe's old nurse Nana enter the room, the Gypsy seems to be menacing Barbe; old Nana leaps forward to attack the Gypsy and is killed by his knife. He is tried for murder and sentenced to fifteen years' imprisonment at hard labor—a fate that, for a wild spirit like his, is far worse than death. Barbe seems willing to keep his wife and children, but they depart suddenly—and at Barbe's door is laid a bundle of the Gypsy's clothes and his hat with its gallant feather.

Barbe's cruelty is so cold and so irrational that she seems at last merely inhuman. For that reason *Gypsy, Gypsy* is somewhat less than successful. The novel form, after all, requires at the very least a sense of life, but in *Gypsy, Gypsy* only the minor characters are endowed with warmth and vitality. Henrietta, like the adolescent twins of *The Lady and the Unicorn*, is budding and passionate; René, nephew of Barbe's late hus-

band, is strong and tender; and many of the lesser characters
are given some range of feeling and motivation.

Madame Barbe, though lifeless and evil herself, is envious
of warmth and purity, like some doomed spirit or vampire. Occasionally this attribute is made all too plain, as when she says
to Henrietta: "I had a dream about you. You were a
statue . . . cold, shining white . . . glossy and naked and I was
standing in front of you with filthy black hands. I kept wiping
them down on you, trying to get some of the blackness off on
you, and not a stain would you take. I thought it was so typical
of you."[1] Although Barbe seems to regret at least a part of the
destruction she causes, she scarcely regrets having brought it
about.

Two similar women in later novels are more believable and
more varied in their emotional range. Louise Pool and Sophie
Barrington Ward make foolish and selfish decisions, but they
live to see their errors and to regret them deeply. Louise Pool
of *Breakfast with the Nikolides* is the wife of Charles Pool,
an agricultural expert at a college in East Bengal, and the mother
of his two daughters, Emily and Binnie. They have lived apart
for eight years when war in Europe forces Louise to bring the
children to India, as Miss Godden herself did in real life. Gradually, the reader learns that Louise left her husband because
he once forced himself upon her. Angry because of this ill usage,
she has refused to correspond with him. They are not especially
glad to be reunited, and Charles's house resembles an armed
camp through most of the book.

The older daughter, Emily, is the center of a great deal of
the action. The title of the novel refers to a meal that she and
her sister Binnie take with a neighboring family while Emily's
little spaniel Don is being destroyed by a veterinarian. The death
of the dog is central to the novel, for Louise makes the decision
without being sure the dog has rabies, and she carries it out
without consulting Emily or Charles. It is typical of her willful,
headstrong character to act so hastily; in fact, the disasters in
the story result directly or indirectly from Louise's hasty speech
and ill-considered action. Having the spaniel killed loses for
Louise the small respect her daughter has held for her. The
grief-ridden Emily mourns for her dog beside a pond where
a youthful Indian poet and college student befriends her; but,

when he takes Emily home, Louise impulsively accuses him of molesting the little girl. He is insulted, and the Indian students riot the next day because of wild rumors that the boy has been violently abused in some way. As if to confirm the rumors, the student dies that very day—but of lockjaw, from a cut inflicted by a piece of rusty metal some time earlier. Emily herself barely escapes injury or death at the hands of the mob.

From this death and fear of death, however, come some hopeful results. At long last, Louise and Charles are able to discuss thoroughly their hurts; and the next day an observer notes that Charles has "singularly the look of a man who has been fed; he had lost a haggardness that he used to have. . . ."[2] Although Emily discovers her mother's treachery in having had the spaniel killed, she has gained an understanding of grief and loneliness that will be of more use to her than innocence. She is growing up, as Rumer and Jon Godden did, by learning that even loved adults are often willful and wrong.

Even when the male is strong, then, an excessively forceful female character can cause trouble as she does in *Breakfast with the Nikolides*. Louise's headstrong acts jeopardize the children's lives and happiness, and only when Louise submits to her husband can a reasonably happy ending occur. This end is not unexpected; earlier in the novel, Louise has submitted to Charles in small matters and has discovered a surprising pleasure in doing so. Neither husband nor wife must dominate, Miss Godden appears to say. Although, in general, the wife should submit to her husband, a mutual respect and forbearance should characterize the marriage relationship.

When the male is weak, of course, the female partner in a marriage may be encouraged to take the initiative. In *Kingfishers Catch Fire* (1953), Sophie Barrington Ward has married a man who is handsome but lacks some unspecified quality of manly strength or will; therefore, Sophie's resolution was stronger than his. When he went to India, she did not accompany him; instead, like Louise Pool and like Miss Godden herself, she brings her two children to India because of the war. Rather than stay with her husband, however, Sophie and her small daughter and son move like nomads around wartime India, without a word of protest from her husband Denzil. When he dies of a cold—weak fellow—Sophie calmly decides to stay in the country and live

economically among the people, for Denzil has left her with
large debts and a tiny pension. That she nearly succeeds in
this dangerous enterprise is to the credit of her independent
spirit and resourcefulness, one gathers; and that she fails in
the end is evidence both of her willfulness and of her masterless
condition.

Like Louise Pool, Sophie cannot seem to reach an understanding with her daughter Teresa; and again like Louise, she brings
upon herself and her family a disaster she cannot foresee. Nevertheless, Sophie and Teresa, like Louise and Emily, grow during
their ordeals. They do not grow much wiser, but their spirits
are richer for a year spent apart from Western society and in
daily contact with simple people and a gorgeous landscape.
Sophie, in order to supplement her small income after her husband's death, teaches "English to Hindu and Mohammedan
ladies, and Urdu to English people."[3] Such tutelage does not
pay well, and her work is long and hard. Presently, she falls
ill, and her daughter summons a doctor from a mission hospital
(operated, it may be noted, by Anglican nuns).

The doctor puts Sophie in the hospital, where she nearly dies
of typhoid and pneumonia. Even when death seems near, however, she can summon no demonstrative love for her child;
Teresa, calling goodnight to her mother, hears her reply: "Good
night—you little—nuisance. Good night."[4] Strengthened by a
blood transfusion given by the young surgeon who has fallen
in love with her, Sophie survives. With her usual disregard for
the conventions and for the sensitivities of others, she decides
that the thing to do is to live as the natives do. Since she has
no money, she cannot live in the customary style of Europeans
in India; to live cheaply, she takes a house named Dhilkusha[5]
near a village in the vale of Kashmir.

There she manages to offend the townspeople, violate the
local customs, and generally make herself troublesome. It is not
that she is ungenerous; indeed, she is so generous that she sets
community elements against each other. She gives her servants
holidays—but their culture understands only unremitting work;
she tries teaching the women to sew, in a society wherein only
men sew and women do only manual labor. Her conduct is
so heedless, and yet her guardian angel so protective, that she
creates disturbances without, at least for a time, suffering any

consequences. As an aunt of hers has said, Sophie somehow "omits the effect." But the aunt also makes a prophecy: "Don't worry, one day it will catch up with her. She will be punished. And the worst part of the punishment . . . is that probably she will punish someone else. . . ."⁶

At Dhilkusha, the punishment comes to Sophie. She has started a business in herbs to make money; though she has little faith in herbals herself, she provides the natives with the remedies they want.⁷ But her cook Sultan, acting on an incautious suggestion of hers, secretly prepares an aphrodisiac—for her. As it turns out, the mixture contains ground glass and belladonna, and she survives only because Sultan can never do anything right: he has ground the glass too fine. But Sophie is not the only one to be punished, as the aunt foresaw. Teresa is trapped and severely beaten by the native children who herd cattle, although Sophie has assured her that they are merely children and cannot hurt her. Nabir, the caretaker of Sophie's house, finds Teresa's senseless body where the native children have hidden it and thereby saves the child's life, but he too is punished in the general retribution by being imprisoned under suspicion of participating in a plot against the English family.

Sophie, however, has become too much a part of her new environment; she cannot bring herself to press charges against Sultan, and she tries to get Nabir released. Her European acquaintances find her attitude appalling, especially since Teresa still lies unconscious and in danger of death. Circumstances become almost too much for even Sophie to override them by sheer force of will. She is injured in attempting, while still quite ill, to secure statements clearing Nabir of blame in the injury of her daughter. But she has succeeded, despite her injury, and is about to collapse when out of a car steps a familiar if fantastic figure—who is also, not at all incidentally, an old friend and former sweetheart: Dr. Toby, who has come all the way from England as if by miracle. He appears like a *deus ex machina,* but no miracle has occurred; Teresa has written Toby a letter before the final crisis, and Sophie finds that she is very glad indeed to have him there.

Even after Toby takes her home as his bride, Sophie cannot feel that her ordeal was too much to bear, as everyone else seems to think; Teresa has won a new independence and courage from her brush with danger and death, and if she still does not respect her mother very much—well, she never has. Sophie cannot regret even her most foolish act, the purchase of a fabulously beautiful and fabulously expensive carpet when she knew she would never be able to pay for it. The message of the book is Sophie's oft-reiterated belief that one does what one must do.

The reader is forced to admire Sophie's headstrong courage, even while he sees most clearly that her acts must bring loss and pain. Character, Miss Godden might have said, grows in difficulty—no less in the difficulty one creates than in that which arrives unbidden. Or, had she wished to speak it directly (instead of indirectly through the poem by Gerard Manley Hopkins, from which her title came), she might have said that people do what comes naturally—as kingfishers cannot help catching the light as they flash through the air.

In contrast to the portrayals of the roles of wives and mothers, Miss Godden presents in Selina Dane of *Take Three Tenses* and Angela Chesney of *An Episode of Sparrows* two women who are intelligent and (at least in public) generous; but they are treated unsympathetically by their creator; and the unproductive lives of these maiden ladies suggest the uselessness of lone women.

Selina's father, the founder of the Dane family home at 99 Wiltshire Place, London, has been a widower for fifteen years when, in 1879, he presents to his daughter, then nearly thirty and unmarried, a seven-year-old girl named Lark Ingoldsby. The child's parents, he says, have just perished in the collapse of the Tay Bridge; he himself was traveling with the child by another train. Lark's mother was an opera singer with a voice so beautiful that John Dane traveled far to hear it; whether he traveled for any other end, and how frequently he did so in the past, are not clear.

Selina naturally suspects something more; but her father merely informs her that Lark is to be brought up as his daughter in his house. Selina treats the child with thinly veiled scorn; and, after John Dane's death, Lark is little better than a servant in the house except in the eyes of Rollo, Selina's younger brother, who loves Lark all his life. That young lady, however, grows up and marries a marchese; but Selina continues to live her empty, pathetic life, alone and unloved, in the family house.

Angela Chesney, on the other hand, does not direct her ill temper against any specific individual, unless it be her shy, retiring older sister, Olivia, who lives with her. Angela, the dominant sister, also seems to dominate the neighborhood in which they live—Mortimer Square, London—and also the boards and charities she serves. And when someone appears to have been stealing earth from the ornamental gardens in the Square, Miss Angela thinks of calling the police; but her more sensitive sister perceives that small children have been taking the earth, for she has noticed a footprint or two. Some "street sparrows," poor children from Catford Street, have started that most unimaginable of projects in their seamy quarter: a garden. Lovejoy Mason, unwanted child of an "actress," has snatched a packet of flower seed; and her possessiveness and her love of beauty have driven her to try to make a garden in the ruins of a bombed-out church. No adult knows about it, and none would understand it—none except Olivia Chesney, whose intuition and perceptions are delicate enough to know even where her eyes have not seen. Angela, unknowing and unwilling to admit her lack of knowledge, would have smashed this delicate enterprise; luck, and Olivia, make it possible for the garden to flourish amid the ruins, and for Lovejoy's spirit to blossom in an otherwise barren, hopeless life.

Both Selina Dane and Angela Chesney are stereotyped characters: the standard, crabbed old maids who, having missed happiness themselves, seemingly cannot permit others to find it. No doubt the rather severe nuns who figure in a number of stories are likewise stereotyped. But Sister Laura Mary, already noted as the superior of an Anglican convent school in the autobiographical story "The Little Fishes,"[8] is a portrait etched in acid; like Sister Clodagh and Sister Malone, she is insensitive to the opinions and feelings of others; but, like Clodagh, she can be brought up short by a word from a superior. Another old maid is similar to these in her businesslike manner and shortness of temper: "Madame" Anna Holbein, mistress of a ballet school in London. Her story, told in *A Candle for St. Jude,* permits her a measure of understanding for other persons. Although she customarily ignores the sensibilities of others, she is able to sympathize with and to admire a rising young dancer,

Hilda French, in whose ambition and restlessness she sees some
reflection of herself. It is worthy of notice, however, that the
author has referred to Madame Holbein as "almost a
'stock figure.'"[9]

II Incompleteness of Women

Whether stereotyped or individualized, the lives of these headstrong women delineate paradoxically one of the major themes
in Rumer Godden's novels and stories: the necessary incomplete-
ness of a woman without a man, her dependence upon masculine
qualities either in herself or in other persons. As examples of
this dependence of the female upon male, Sophie, despite her
impatience with her ineffectual husband, is after his death like
a storm-blown ship that has snapped its mooring cable: even
after Toby appears, Sophie struggles for two years against being
brought to anchorage beside him. Louise Pool arrogantly refuses
her husband the marriage bed, thereby winning separation and
pain for her daughters and for herself; forced by the war to
rejoin her husband, she still inflicts pain but nevertheless finds
her proper place in bringing fulfillment to Charles and the
chance of security to her daughters.

Even with husbands and even with the best intentions, Miss
Godden's women often make foolish decisions. Two who manage
to wreak havoc with the happiness of their families, and who
do so with the least possible malice, are Mrs. Grey of *The Greengage Summer* (1958) and Fanny Clavering of *The Battle of
the Villa Fiorita* (1963). Mrs. Grey comes of a solid middle-class
English family (characteristically named Bullock), but she is
married to a botanist who goes away on three-year expeditions
and scarcely gives a thought to his family. The children, therefore, arrive at intervals of three years; and Mother herself is
like one of them, another child. They live for a time in a house
belonging to her older brother, William Bullock, but presently
Mrs. Grey decides that the five children must not be permitted
to grow up without having seen the battlefields in France; somewhat obscurely, she considers those sights an antidote for the
selfishness she believes to be developing in her offspring.

As in other stories of Miss Godden's, the selfishness is the
protagonist's own. And so, predictably, Mrs. Grey becomes ill
in France, just as Sophie did in India; and the Grey children,

like Sophie's, are left to the mercies of strangers while she is in the hospital. That they survive at all is lucky enough; but that their mother's wish for them should be fulfilled in spite of herself is little less than miraculous. For they do indeed learn to be less selfish; and, more to the point, they become 'far more aware of the world around them.

Joss, the oldest, is dazzled by a romantic Englishman who lives in the Hôtel des Oeillets at Vieux-Moutiers where the children have been lodged; when he turns out to be a desperado, all the children are shocked. Cecil, the narrator, has envied the maturity of her older sister; but, during their "greengage summer," she becomes a woman, too—without the help of her mother to tell her what is happening. Hester, William (called "Willmouse"), and Vicky, who turns five that summer, all experience evil in some way that contributes to their growth toward adulthood. Their lives are actually in peril, for the English murderer Eliot is the only grownup who seems to care for their welfare at all—until little Willmouse becomes a real threat to Eliot's safety. When things look darkest, however, Uncle William (solid, middle class, and dependably English) arrives at a crucial juncture—just as Dr. Toby did in *Kingfishers Catch Fire*. In fact, he comes just as Toby did—in response to an urgent message that is kept secret from most of the participants in the story until his arrival. Presumably Mrs. Grey will regret their ordeal no more than Sophie regretted Teresa's. Mrs. Grey's feelings, however, are not explored, and so *The Greengage Summer* remains a more superficial and less probable treatment of the themes already treated in *Kingfishers Catch Fire*.

A similar failure of the masculine principle appears to be the cause of the Claverings' divorce in *The Battle of the Villa Fiorita*. Fanny has been too independent, with her husband away at the royal court so much and, when he is at home, so unassertive. Therefore, in Miss Godden's terms, when Rob Quillet, an attractive and assertive man, does arrive, he sweeps Fanny off her feet with scarcely an effort and carries her away, after the divorce, to an Italian villa. Fanny is the last person to have thought herself capable of such an action; she is rather an ordinary woman, not considered exceptional in beauty, intellect, or charm; and, although the reader is not permitted a deep look into her heart except in regard to her lover, it is fairly clear that she loves her children: Philippa, Hugh, and Caddie. But she is immensely, unthinkingly selfish; when her two younger children, Hugh and Caddie, run away and cross the Continent to visit her in Italy, she is neither abashed nor angry but smugly triumphant: "Indeed, she felt blessed more than she deserved: to have Rob and this warm triumph in her heart: 'They ran away. They ran away to me.' "[10]

She does not, in fact, marry Rob Quillet as she has expected to do, but that is not because of any sudden realization that she loves her children and her husband; it is because the three children (her two younger ones and Rob's daughter by an earlier marriage) plague and embarrass both Fanny and Rob in public, so that even in Italy, where a certain tolerance might be expected for a private liaison, the affair begins to attract public censure. The children go on a hunger strike at home; Caddie appeals to an Italian priest in a nearby town to make her mother a Catholic—so she cannot be divorced, or, being divorced, cannot remarry; and Hugh and Pia, Rob's daughter, are all but killed in a sailing accident. A grand passion clearly cannot stand before the force of a child's filial determination.

In all these stories, the lordly male is the ideal husband and protector of foolish or headstrong females. An Indian couple in *Breakfast with the Nikolides* suggests even more specifically Miss Godden's view of the proper relationship between man and wife. Narayan Das, a young veterinary surgeon, is determinedly modern and progressive; but his wife Shila is docile and submissive in the old style. His progressiveness does not extend, however, to a real concern for his wife's feelings; he neglects her to spend time with his friend Anil, a student at the nearby agricultural college. And shortly before the birth of their first child he acknowledges that he is sufficiently old-fashioned to be very proud if the baby should be a son. Naturally, the subservience of wives to their husbands is not without its wrongs. Even though Rumer Godden disparages the willfulness of unattached women, she has frequently stressed the essential cruelty of marital relationships by portraying wives whose spirits are repressed or crushed by insensitive husbands.

The young urban wife in the story "Why Not Live Sweetly?"[11] longs for her old home in the country; for she resents all the "conveniences" in the so-called mansion flat where she lives with her journalist husband who tries to teach her the virtue of adaptability. She finds her justification, although a bitter one, in a poem that she remembers from school. Not identified in the story itself, this poem is Keats's song "I had a dove," and it is the source of both the theme and the title:

> I had a dove and the sweet dove died;
> And I have thought it died of grieving:
> O, what could it grieve for? Its feet were tied,
> With a silken thread of my own hand's weaving;
> Sweet little red feet! why should you die—
> Why should you leave me, sweet bird! why?
> You liv'd alone in the forest-tree,
> Why, pretty thing! would you not live with me?
> I kissed you oft and gave you white peas;
> Why not live sweetly, as in the green trees?[12]

Like Griselda Dane of *Take Three Tenses*, like the "mousewife" in the children's book of that title, and like poor Penny Stevens of *In This House of Brede*—like these three, this young wife is seen as a wild spirit bound cruelly to a not unkind but thoroughly selfish and materialistic husband. (One recalls in this connection Rumer's remark that she did not love her own father, who indulged himself with dogs and guns but does not appear to have denied his family.[13]) Unlike those three, the young wife in "Why Not Live Sweetly?" yearns for freedom not so much from her housekeeping as from the particular place where she dwells; her old country home is shown as her natural environment; lacking it, she must pine and die.

Not all women resemble wild birds, however, and Rumer Godden has also given her readers a fine story about a girl who goes willingly enough, though forced by custom, to the captivity of her new home and bridegroom. There is scarcely any more touching tale of first love and marriage, and none truer, than her story "The Red Doe."[14] In it, young Ibrahim, with friends and relations, visits a distant tribe to negotiate for a bride whom he has never met and who returns home with him the same day. With the lightest, surest strokes, the author delineates the masculine pride, the youthful reluctance of the bridegroom, his selfishness that melts with a look at the strange girl who is already at his mercy, and the beginnings of tenderness and devotion that underlie the marital customs of every civilized people. With still fewer strokes, Miss Godden has drawn in the bride a hesitance and yearning that must be ingrained in the memory of the human race, so familiar they seem.

As the death of the captive dove was symbolic of the wife's dying spirit in "Why Not Live Sweetly?," so the death of another animal represents the wife's utter dependence upon her husband in "The Red Doe." On the return journey with his bride, Ibrahim passes a certain glade and recalls the end of a chase that had occurred there earlier. He had leaped from his horse to cut the throat of a doe that lay with a spear through its neck: "He remembered himself bending down with the knife in his hand and he remembered that the doe, with the blood gushing from her wound, had looked at him and then he was alone with her. No father, no Jassoof, no others were with him then. It was only Ibrahim and the doe, and he—he saw it in her eyes—had done this to her. And suddenly, it was he who was stricken, not the doe, because he was not Ibrahim, himself, any more. He was Ibrahim and the doe."[15]

After the marriage feast with her new husband's tribe, Ibrahim's bride, modestly veiled and robed, is led out to him and mounted upon a pony. Accidentally, as he holds her pony, his hand touches her thigh; startled, he presses harder until something falls on the back of his hand: a tear. Momentarily his resolution wavers, but presently he rides away with his bride, already a new man: "he knew that he could not be only Ibrahim again . . . he knew that what had started in him with the doe was in him with the tear and would be in him now forever."[16]

Thus, in crucial times of birth or death, marriage or divorce, Rumer Godden's characters, especially the women, discover that their lives are no longer entirely free but are and must be bound inextricably to other lives. Griselda Dane of *Take Three Tenses* longs for a vacation trip to exotic places; but her husband, described as wise and genuinely kind, always gets his way: they always go to Scotland so that he can fish. Moreover, although Griselda feels already quite burdened with six children, John is determined that they shall have *nine*. He smiles gently at her when she complains, but they go to Scotland, and they do have nine children. The domineering male triumphs—but Griselda dies at the birth of the ninth child. With her accustomed delicacy, Rumer Godden does not comment on the pathos of Griselda's death, nor does she stress the kind brutality of John Dane.

That, it seems clear, is in the novelist's view the way things are, if not the way they should be: the husband, lordly; the wife, submissive. In fact, she has spelled out her feeling (although in another context) on the difference between the sexes in a reflective and autobiographical work, *Thus Far and No Further:*

I never long to be a man so much as in my writings; to be a man, because I should have a man's wholeness. To me that is what a woman can never have; I think she can never be whole. . . . She must be continually impaired . . . drained, as she is drained by her menses each month. Complete wholeness is male, a woman cannot hope to achieve it. . . . To the extent that she is masculine she approaches it, to the extent that a man is feminine he loses it, but men have this robust easy power and they do not even know they have it; it is an unconscious lordliness.[17]

Modernity, then, in the marital relation holds no charm for Rumer Godden, if it means absolute equality; rather, modernity is to be avoided in favor of wifely submission to the will of her husband. The wife will know how to get her own way sometimes, but she will be satisfied to give the husband his, or seem to, in general. A woman's lot, to judge by the novels and stories, is to weep and to endure, as well as to keep house; but her life can be made even more difficult by her husband's abdication of his seignorial rights. Modernity, in fact, is no more to be desired in one's marriage than in one's house; and, in the matter of family homes, Miss Godden has consistently plumped for the tried and true, the traditional, even if that is utterly conventional.

III   *A Nun, a Prince, a Chimney Sweep*

Quite a different reflection of the same attitudes may be seen in *In This House of Brede.* In this novel, the tried and true is religious faith, and the tradition is one of the oldest in the Western world: Christian monasticism. The protagonist, Philippa Talbot, a widow who has had to make her own way in the world, has succeeded so well that to her friends—indeed, to everyone who meets her—she seems superior, born to lead and to take responsibility. It is not only her native ability, nor yet her husbandless condition, that has made her domineering, of course; for, like Miss Godden's lordly males, Philippa enjoys a position of command at least partly because others have allowed her to dominate them. But like them—this point is a crucial one— like those lordly males and the foolish women represented by Sophie Barrington Ward, Philippa finds that dominance is a lonely condition.

One day by chance she enters a Catholic church; almost by accident she joins the line waiting to enter the confessional; and thus begins a series of religious experiences, none of them specified in the novel, which culminate in Philippa's entering Brede Abbey as a Benedictine postulant. Hard as her life there is, she believes she has found solace for her loneliness and relief from her sin of arrogance. It is years before she discovers that her pride has only been hidden by the habit, and it is many months more before she can yield it freely in exchange for love and grace. As a bride of Christ, she had been unconsciously incomplete until she made that final surrender of self. But desire alone, discipline alone, prayer alone did not cause that surrender; altogether, they only made it possible. The connection between Philippa's story and those of Sister Clodagh, Sophie, and Mrs. Grey is no accident. Yielding one's self to the lordship of another, whether God or man, is one alternative to the loneliness and unconscious arrogance of independence. Even if that lordship is only the discipline of a craft or calling, it represents security and hope for the future.

In two short articles, "The Eternal Severities" and "A Prince for All Seasons," Miss Godden has given her readers not only some more examples of her adherence to the traditional and the conventional but also some reasons for her adherence. The first article emphasizes the recurrent war between the genera- tions: children may rebel against the strictures of their parents, but they grow up to restrain their own offspring in similar ways, though perhaps from opposite reasons. Loving parents may try to soften life's buffets, to make things easier in order that their children might be "happier." But regulation, if it grows from love, is not excessive; it is really excess (whether of restraint or freedom) rather than regulation that is evil. Aristotle, she says, "if he were only easier to read—is the perfect philosopher for the nursery" because he helps one to find the mean, "the middle way between excess and deficiency."[18] Thus Sophie in *Kingfishers Catch Fire* and Mrs. Grey in *The Greengage Summer* act as willfully as spoiled children; they are so irresponsible indeed that their young daughters are forced to act the adult role.

In both those novels, as this study has already demonstrated, the conflicts are resolved by the introduction of strong, no-nonsense men. Thus it comes as no surprise to discover, in the second article, that Miss Godden warmly admires Prince Philip as the very model of masculine enthusiasm and strength of body and mind. The Prince's vigor, his energetic pursuit of excellence, the fullness of his active life—all these seem to Rumer Godden (as wife, mother, and grandmother) appropriate and complete counterbalances to the boredom and emptiness professed by many young persons today. As a model husband, father, and man-among-men, Philip has Miss Godden's wholehearted endorsement in "A Prince for All Seasons."[19]

Rather at the other extreme in the social scale, and a representative of the opposite sex, is the subject of another article, who likewise has the novelist's hearty admiration for finding true freedom and mastery in devotion to the discipline of work. Mrs. Abel, the village chimney sweep and layer-out of the dead (as well as "The Most Unforgettable Character I've Met"), does not regard either occupation as demeaning at all: "It's only another kind of cleaning up."[20] Cheerful and independent, Mrs. Abel knows her own mind, does her work swiftly and well, and in being her own hearty self cleans far more than chimneys: "Behind her she leaves such a sense of well-being that the house seems radiant—an odd word, perhaps, for chimney sweeping, but not if it is the homely warm radiance of firelight, for instance."[21]

Small wonder that Rumer Godden put Mrs. Abel into not one but two of her novels, *China Court* and *In This House of Brede*. Knowing Mrs. Abel, the reader of all the novels may better understand the sense they convey of housewifely order, of tidying up, of wayward things being set to rights. Security in the midst of change is possible in the world of Rumer·Godden—possible if one obeys the laws of God and nature, and if he acknowledges change as a natural, inevitable part of that order. If "time is a stream," as Miss Godden indicated in one of her stories, and if mankind is caught up in that swift stream, it is as well to build oneself a raft. Discipline, ceremony, imagination, good sense, moderation, and regular activity—these are the materials of which rafts are made. The message is clear at last—a woman may need a raft more than a man does, for her nature is less suited than his to the excesses of independence.

CHAPTER 4

The River of Time

RUMER Godden's characters, though generally self-centered, are sometimes struck with a frustrating sense of their own insignificance. Especially striking in their consciousness of the vast sweep of events are the children and young people cast adrift, as it were, in space and time. "That is just it," says Harriet in *The River,* wondering why things have not stopped with the sudden death of her little brother. "It happens, and then things come round again, begin again, and you can't stop them. They go on happening, whatever happens."[1] And she composes a poem on that theme, though she has tried to tell herself she can never write again:

> The river runs, the round world spins.
> Dawn and lamplight. Midnight. Noon.
> Sun follows day. Night, stars and moon.
> The day ends, the end begins.[2]

I Take Three Tenses

Rumer Godden's first *roman-fleuve* was *Take Three Tenses* (1945, called in England *A Fugue in Time*). The first two of its four epigraphs are important chiefly as they deal with techniques employed in the novel, particularly the mingling of past, present, and future events. The first epigraph quotes Lawrence Abbott's description of Bach's fugues as "two, three, or four simultaneous melodies . . . constantly on the move." Such contrapuntal relationships (as in Aldous Huxley's *Point Counter Point* [1928]) are analogous to the intermingled stories of several generations of the Dane family, and the glances forward in time are to be explained as completing a harmonic pattern: "Often chords are incomplete; only two tones are sounded so that one's imagination has to fill in the missing third tone."

T. S. Eliot's "East Coker" is the source of the second epigraph. Old General Dane has found in it both strength and justification; "Home is where one starts from" and

> We must be still and still moving
> Into another intensity
> For a further union, a deeper communion. . . .
> . . . In my end is my beginning.

But if General Dane finds his justification in the second of Eliot's *Four Quartets*, Miss Godden must have found both her theme and her technique in the opening lines of the first, "Burnt Norton":

> Time present and time past
> Are both perhaps present in time future,
> And time future contained in time past.

> . . .

> Time past and time future
> What might have been and what has been
> Point to one end, which is always present.

The other two epigraphs, drawn from *The Book of Common Prayer*, establish the themes of the swiftness of time, the brevity of life, and the poignance of birth and of youth: "Man that is born of woman hath but a short time to live" and "Like as arrows in the hand of a giant even so are the young children."

Take Three Tenses is divided into six sections, five of them with consecutive temporal names: Morning, Noon, Four O'Clock, Evening, and Night. It is the story of one century in the life of a London house. The inhabitants are important chiefly in the aggregate, for the family history repeats itself, and the house becomes the sum of all the lives it has sheltered: "The house, it seems, is more important than the characters," runs the first sentence. " 'In me you exist,' says the house."[3]

The Dane family has held a ninety-nine year lease on Number 99 Wiltshire Place. Now, in 1940, the lease is about to expire, to the sorrow of old General Sir Roland Ironmonger Dane, who lives there alone with his memories and one faithful retainer. Like other fictional houses, this one holds all that is valued by its elderly occupant. "In the house the past is present,"[4] and the present only repeats the past in a cycle of love and jealousy, birth and death. The life of the family and of the house is a succession of butlers, of generations in the nursery, of dogs and cats, of children's songs and stories, of provisions bought and meals prepared and eaten, of candlelight, gaslight, and electric light—the last installed in the house by General Dane himself because he "didn't want it to miss anything"[5]

It has not missed anything of importance, to judge by the "house voices" that speak in apparently random order. It is a garrulous old building, and its function of memory resembles a sort of chronic total recall:

> *"I am the house dog."*
> *"I am the house cat."*
> *"Chick chick chick chick chick chick."*
> *"Take three tenses."* [voices, real and imagined, from the past]
> *"And last of all, before we say 'Good night,' to Verity Dane of London . . ."* [voice of radio announcer, referring to a future occupant of the house]
> *"You are beautiful. Beautiful."*
> *"You understand about the soubise?"*
> *"John, how do you pronounce Popocatepetl?"*
> *"Can't he get boots in Worcestershire?"* [voices from the past]
> *"When you said 'All right,' you meant all right for flying didn't you?"* [voice from the present][6]

This passage demonstrates that what the house recalls is not all past action. Some of the "house voices" are from the immediate present and some actually from the future. The novelist constantly, and with no warning, shifts backward and forward in a period of a hundred years (one hundred and seven, counting the glimpses into futurity), so that reading the book is a real challenge. Yet *Take Three Tenses* does not approach the difficulty of some other contemporary novels, for Rumer Godden has laid a trail of clues and dates that make a chronological reconstruction fairly simple. Not all of her clues are helpful, it is true; Selina Dane is said to have been born both in

June and in December,[7] and the future "Verity Dane" is presumably the son of a man surnamed Masterson. But in the main,
a patient reader can have no serious difficulty with events in
the story.

Some degree of patience is required, however, to discover
that verb tenses are employed not in conventional fashion but
as devices to reinforce the general theme that the past is continually present in an old family dwelling, and also that present
action is being stored up as already past. Thus, in the year
of the main or present action—1940—the past tense describes
contemporary events, while present tense is employed for older
times (italics added): "*Now* in the meat cage in the larder
were only the crops, the ration for Proutie and Rolls, for half
a week. It *looked* strangely empty. It *is* accustomed to hold,
in Mrs. Proutie's time, for one day, perhaps a dozen sausages
on a plate; a leg of mutton [and so on for a food catalogue
running nearly a full page]. . . ."[8]

Contrasting wartime scarcity with former plenty, this passage
with its inverted tenses is clear enough to the reader who already
knows that Mrs. Proutie was the cook for forty-seven years,
beginning in 1841 when the house was new, and that her elderly
nephew Proutie is the single manservant now, 1940. Present
tense is not only for past action but also for the future:
" 'Gravel?' *says* little Verity, Rolls's great-great-nephew in the
bad winter of *nineteen forty-seven* [the novel was published
in 1945]. 'Gravel? It isn't gravel, it is grapenuts'."[9] A kind of
historical present tense, then, is employed for both past and
future time, while past tense represents present action.

No doubt this summation oversimplifies a fairly complex narrative pattern, but the pattern is surely not quite so complex
as Professor John R. Frey found. In a 1947 article, Frey discovered three major patterns of tense in the novel: first, "the combination of imperfect and present for the main action and in relation to them the perfect and past perfect for the flashback";
second, "from the depiction of incidents in the distant
past . . . where incidents are presented in their own right, so
to speak . . . she again operates with the flashback, employing
for it the imperfect, the perfect, the past perfect, and even the
present"; and, finally, "the description of such future scenes [as
those involving little Verity] and in relation to it again the flash-

back in the perfect constitutes the third unit in the tense pattern. . . ."[10]

Of course, as Professor Frey noted, it was nothing new for a novelist to shift time levels; but a "corresponding shift of tenses like that undertaken by Miss Godden . . . signifies a complete and perhaps questionable innovation." Nevertheless, he pointed out, the novel had been received favorably in the main, and that reception was "most significant," perhaps heralding a "breakdown in traditional treatment of the tenses"[11]—a prediction as yet unfulfilled.

The favorable reception was significant, but probably the reception of her novel owed much to the relief it affords from the tortuous convolutions of contemporary stream-of-consciousness fiction. Rumer Godden's strikingly different use of verb tenses was accepted, surely, because it provided a helpful key to understanding the stratified experience within the Dane house, and not because of a general public willingness to blur the distinctions among grammatical tenses.

In any case, the apparent relaxation in *Take Three Tenses* of conventional means of indicating temporal relations has the effect of cutting loose the reader and setting him adrift in time. By no coincidence, that effect exactly parallels the theme of *Take Three Tenses:* the streamlike quality of family life, and the consequent feeling of continuity that surrounds a dwelling long occupied by members of the same family. As Orville Prescott states, when writing of this novel and of the similar *China Court,* "All that living and dying, loving and grieving, all that daily routine, cannot be lost forever. Some of it must permeate the house itself so that time itself dissolves and everything goes on at once."[12]

Everything does, indeed, go on at once. What goes on, first of all, is that John Dane brings his bride Griselda in October, 1841, into the new house at 99 Wiltshire Place, where they produce nine children in twenty-two years; but Griselda dies at the birth of the last one, Roland, born in December, 1863. In 1940, the present, the only Dane living there is that same Roland (called Roly as a child, Rollo in young manhood, and Rolls as a mature man). General Dane is embittered at being forced to retire from the British army during wartime.

Suddenly one day a visitor appears—an American girl in uni-

form; and she is Grizel Dane, granddaughter of Roland's oldest
brother, Pelham, who had settled in the United States.[13] She is
looking for a comfortable place to stay, scarcely interested in
the house except as she has a claim to shelter in it; old General
Dane grumpily prefers his own society, but stay Grizel does;
and a tentative but warm bond develops between old man and
young girl. Presently another visitor arrives, a young British
airman called Pilot Officer Masterson. He turns out also to be
an Italian marchese, but that is not the strangest thing about
him. The strangest is that, although he has never been in the
house before, he knows as much about it as if he had been an
occupant. He knows because he has been there *in spirit;* as
a child, he was told stories about the house by Lark, his aunt
by marriage, who had grown up in the Dane household.

Lark Ingoldsby had not been a Dane, however, unless indeed
she was a natural child of John Dane, whose wife had died
nine years before Lark's birth in November, 1872. Lark had
first come, as has been mentioned earlier, to the house when
she was seven. Her mother, an opera singer adored by John
Dane, had just died with her husband in the Tay Bridge disaster
when John Dane brought the child home to his daughter Selina,
a spinster of twenty-nine, declining to say, of the child's relationship to the family, more than that she was to be reared as
Selina's "sister." Her natural resentment and her own harsh character did not fit Selina to treat the child kindly, so Lark grew
up as a sort of unwanted stepchild; apparently John Dane, because of her mother, could not bear to think of her—just as
the death of his wife had also raised a barrier between him
and Roland, the son whose birth was Griselda's death. There-
after, at any rate, John Dane scarcely appears in the story.

Despite her handicaps, Lark is a beautiful and charming
woman at eighteen, beloved of Pelham, the oldest son, and of
Roland, the youngest. She seems really to love Roland, but he
cannot live on his pay, much less support a wife; and she cannot
endure life with Selina now that John Dane is dead. Fortunately,
she does not have to do so; for an Italian marchese is also
in love with her; so she marries him and goes to live in Italy
for the rest of her life.

But the pledges of love between Lark and Roland are too
strong to be broken utterly; when, in old age, he retires to the

Dane house, he finds more than memories of Lark—he finds her voice, her presence, and with that presence he carries on intimate dialogues as if he and Lark had been together, not separated, for fifty years. For some months this dialogue has continued when Grizel and, later, Pax Masterson appear on the scene. The General lately has been aware of a small, *very* dark child—the spirit of Pax in boyhood?—moving through the house; presumably, Lark's stories were so vivid that Pax as a child had "lived" in the halls and rooms which he did not actually see until grown up, and where his son Verity (only *slightly* darker than the rest of the Danes) was later to live.

The grand passion of Lark and Rollo is evidently far grander in retrospect than in actuality. By the time Rollo came to notice her as a woman, Lark was grown very tall, full-bodied, and very beautiful; and Rollo's brother Pelham and the Marchese Zacca del Laudi were as smitten as he was himself. Thus the brief moments of declaration between Lark and Rollo, as he remembers them, are like vignettes from some romantic opera— he, handsome and brilliant in an officer's court uniform, standing at the fireplace with a gleaming boot on the fender; she, gorgeously robed and bejeweled. All the grubby facts of Lark's childhood in the house, all the drab realities of the General's later retirement there, all are redeemed and made complete by such flashes of drama and beauty. "One's imagination" (in Lawrence Abbott's words) "has to fill in the missing third tone" in General Dane's life—and in the life of his old house.

Now the meaning of the fantasy becomes clear: old passions, whether vain or not, are enriched and ennobled by memory; the river of time flows on, but it bears ever more human experience. For those like Rumer Godden who possess the sensitive eye and ear and heart, none of that experience is lost forever— none that is worth saving:

> Time past and time future
> What might have been and what has been
> Point to one end, which is always present.

The shifts in time are of no importance; the tenses are merely guideposts when one accepts the permanent availability of past and future as well as present. Here is the importance of *Take*

Three Tenses, its unique blend of imagination and technique, skillfully harmonizing subject and style.

Now it is possible to understand what Miss Godden had vainly sought to achieve in *The Lady and the Unicorn:* some blending of reality and fantasy that would suggest the transforming power of passion. The shadowy bride who haunted the old house in Calcutta was herself deeply unhappy, to judge by the sound of her weeping; but the experience of seeing and hearing her touched the drab life of Rosa Lemarchant with transforming magic.

II   China Court *and "Time Is a Stream"*

Take Three Tenses, then, was not Rumer Godden's first book dealing with an old house haunted by the spirits of former occupants; *The Lady and the Unicorn* had already attempted a treatment of that theme in an Indian setting, and so had *Black Narcissus,* to a lesser extent. Nor did she stop after a second and third treatment. With a grand disregard for those readers who might object to reading approximately the same story three or four times, she proceeded to construct, in *China Court* (1961), a second fictional English dwelling and to establish in it a second prosperous family.

Like the Dane house, China Court was built in 1840; both houses shelter the members of one middle-class family through five generations and for more than a century, and both are filled with "house voices" from their past. Like John and Griselda Dane of 99 Wiltshire Place, Eustace and Adza Quin of China Court have nine children; two Quin children (and two Dane children) die of diphtheria in the same year; only one of the Quin children, a son, has children of his own—and only one of the Danes passed on his name; a youthful American, a great-great-granddaughter of the first Quin (like a great-granddaughter of the first Dane), arrives at the old house just in time to receive it as a legacy from the last survivor who can remember its founders. And, at the end of both novels, the American heiress, allying herself with the scion of a noble family, is to carry on the traditions of the house and to add to them her own experiences, rich at least in anticipation.

Moreover, the widowed Mrs. Quin closely resembles the widowed Mrs. Throckmorton of "Time Is a Stream,"[14] a short story published in 1949, twelve years before *China Court* and four years after *Take Three Tenses*. In spite of herself, Mrs. Throckmorton is forced to acknowledge that in this life "there is no abiding." Assisted by her daughter Eunice, she is leaving the family home because it is too large to maintain on her reduced income. During the packing, Mrs. Throckmorton takes down a book and reads aloud: "Time is a rushing torrent, a stream, fed by life and its changes. One thing sweeps into sight and is swept away. . . ." Later, in a hotel room, the truth of this idea is borne in on her: "I want to think of it. I like it. 'No abiding,' said Mrs. Throckmorton, on the hotel pillows. . . . "That is the healing, in the end. Go back to sleep, Eunice. There is nothing you can do for me. I am glad."[15]

Mrs. Throckmorton's resemblance to Mrs. Quin of *China Court* is far more than coincidence. Each widow lost her only son in World War II; each has several daughters; and the daughters are callous modernists, perfectly willing to see the old house go out of the family and to lose whatever associations are held in the word "home." The proper names Anne, Damaris, McLeod, Eustace, and Stace (or Stacey) are common to both narratives. And, since "Time Is a Stream" was published in 1949 and *China Court* in 1961, the short story may be regarded as a preliminary exercise for Rumer Godden's second novel about the importance of the substantial family home.

Why, one wonders, was it necessary to treat the same themes, names, and persons two or three times? A partial answer may be that the later novel is far more richly elaborated than the earlier one. While the families treated are about the same size, and while the period covered is only slightly greater in *China Court*, the second book runs to more than one hundred thousand words as against seventy-five thousand for *Take Three Tenses*. Despite the complexity of its arrangements, the earlier novel, in comparison, seems sketchy to some readers; and the later one, considered alone, more satisfying and full.

A better explanation of the puzzling repetition is that Mrs. Throckmorton and Eunice *are* Rumer Godden's mother and Rumer herself—and that Mrs. Quin is simply one more attempt to set painful personal memories at rest. "In the short story Mrs. Quin is called Mrs. Throckmorton, but both characters have much in them of my mother. . . . It fell to me, at that

time the only daughter in England, to help with the move and
I had to witness my mother torn away from this home she
loved. . . . After the long distressing day I went to . . . the
hotel. . . . It was then I picked up a book from a pile I had
salvaged . . . I opened it at that quotation: 'Time is a stream
in which there is no abiding.' "[16]

China Court opens with the death of Mrs. Quin in the present,
which is August, 1960. Though not a Quin herself (like Lark,
she was of doubtful parentage and had been a poor orphan),
she had married a grandson of the family's founders, and the
present Quin descendants are all her own. For years it has
seemed that she is the last person to care about the country
house that has sheltered them, for her only son died at Anzio
in World War II, and her daughters are urban and modern
to the last degree. And so, with her death, it seems that the
old Cornish house (named China Court not for the sea trade
that established the family fortune, nor yet for the rose-famille
porcelain, but for the unromantic china-clay works that is the
family's chief enterprise) must gather its voices and spirits and
prepare to be sold. Gradually, the history of the family is revealed, and a rich and varied one it is.

Like its predecessor of some years earlier, *China Court* plays
hob with conventional verb tenses. On the whole, the plan is
the same as in *Take Three Tenses:* present tenses indicate the
distant past in the Quin family, while past tenses are for contemporary events—that is, those in 1960. The transitions are
smoother and less noticeable, perhaps because less frequent.
Moreover, Rumer Godden provided a little introductory note
in which she explained that it takes time to know the members
of a large family: "I believe if the reader is a little patient—and
can bear not to skip—they will soon become distinct and he
will have no need to look at the family tree on the endpapers."
For she has also provided a Quin family tree (see Appendix
B)—a device that might have helped with the Danes in the
earlier *roman-fleuve*.[17]

Like *Take Three Tenses*, *China Court* is marked into temporal
divisions of the day; the chief difference is that the former novel
called them "Morning," "Evening," and so on, while the latter
employs the hours of the religious day, beginning with Lauds,
and going on through Prime, Tierce, Sext, None, Vespers, Com-

pline, and Matins. That is not to say that the earlier book was
secular and the later one religious; neither novel takes a definite
position, and neither fictional family is very religious, though
each attends church and says prayers. Rather, the religious hours
division finds its origin in two Books of Hours that Mrs. Quin
has read for years, especially in her last months. Though she
is not Catholic but Anglican, the books are a comfort to her,
and her housekeeper Cecily (who is strict "chapel" herself),
finds it fitting that Mrs. Quin should use such a "prayerbook."
And it is indeed fitting, not only for spiritual reasons, but also
because the books came into China Court by a strange circumstance in the last century.

In order to understand that circumstance, it is necessary to
go back in time for a bit. Eustace and Adza Quin had nine
children, but only one son carried on the name: Jared married
"Lady Patrick," a proud Irish patrician who bore him two sons,
Borowis and John Henry. Jared was weak and indolent and
had a taste for low women; after his wife found him asleep
in her own bed with a servant girl, she refused to be his wife;
but she lived a painful existence in his family home because
she could not leave her little sons and because she was too
proud to return to her own family. Jared's older sister, who
also shared their home, acted as a paid housekeeper for her
brother as she had done for their father following their mother's
death.

This older sister, Eliza, was everything Jared should have
been and was not: intelligent, clever, eager to manage and to
make. But the Victorian times were against her; she was kept
at home as a child, taught only the rudiments of letters and
numbers, and forbidden to engage in any more businesslike activity than managing the large house. Isolated from eligible
young men, deliberately undereducated, thwarted in her attempts to employ her talents in the quarry business, and frustrated at every turn, she became eccentric, even freakish.

One satisfaction Eliza had, however. Her father employed
as a clerk one Jeremy Baxter, formerly a fellow of Trinity College
but now reduced to working for Quin because he "drank." Baxter
possessed the first—indeed, almost the only—intellectual mind
she knew, and she absorbed his every word. Among other things,
she learned what Baxter understood and her father did not:

that the house contained a number of very valuable old books, bought in a lot by Eustace Quin and simply stored there. Baxter took a perverse satisfaction in keeping his knowledge of their value to himself, but Eliza came to share this attitude. He guided Eliza in her study of books and ideas, and she in return provided him with whisky. Presently Eliza was surreptitiously buying rare books for herself. Being a bibliophile is an expensive business, and she found it expedient to alter the household account books to conceal the fact that she was stealing, first from her father and later from her brother Jared.

After Baxter's death, the legend of Eliza's strangeness grew in the village. She had long been noted for her frugality and her invariable threadbare costume, and she was now suspected of being a witch, for she was seen visiting the graveyard at night. The family nurse Polly followed her one night and watched her light a lantern hidden under her cloak. Kneeling by a grave, Eliza held up books one by one. "Showing books to Jeremy Baxter," said Jared later. "She was mad." Lady Patrick knew better: "She wasn't mad. She was lonely."[18] But this insight came only after Eliza's mysterious death. The scandal of altered accounts uncovered afterward was embarrassing, but Jared found the stubborn strength to face the community, and Eliza was laid to rest honorably with her family. The loneliness of Eliza is pathetic—and so is that of Lady Patrick, her brother's wife. But the isolation that comes to Mrs. Quin when her children and husband are gone is a richly satisfying solitude, and her satisfaction is instructive as to Rumer Godden's purposes, one of which is to demonstrate the unfaithfulness of most persons.

Mrs. Quin's garden is a perpetual solace, and its flowers are more dependable than people. After all, her father-in-law Jared was notoriously unfaithful, and his elder son had betrayed Mrs. Quin herself when, as "Ripsie" (Deborah Russell), she was young and deeply in love with him; and she had married the younger son John Henry, it seems, only because she lost Borowis. Like Lark, who in *Take Three Tenses* retained her feeling for Rollo even when married to another man, Mrs. Quin seems always to have loved Borowis (like Rollo, a handsome young officer); and, long after both men are dead, she can still feel pangs of jealousy when she recalls her successful rival. John

Henry alone among the Quin males is always faithful. Even his son Stace goes his own way, but he is betrayed in his turn by his wife Barbara, an American actress. And the Quin daughters (Bella and three younger girls, so little individualized that they are called only The Three Graces) have almost nothing in common with their mother; they marry husbands as different from her as they are themselves, so that on family occasions they all seem to Mrs. Quin like strangers in her house.

This was not the first time Rumer Godden had touched on the subject of unfaithfulness in personal relationships; it is in fact a familiar motif in her stories and novels. She is realist enough despite the romanticism of some of her resolutions to see that, as there are no ideal persons, so there can be no ideal personal relations. "You must remember," she remarked in *Thus Far and No Further*, "that people do not usually keep their promises. You must not expect it. Think how difficult it is to keep your own and then you will see how unlikely it is that they will keep theirs."[19]

So Mrs. Quin learns from Eliza and her own experience that "loneliness can be good."[20] It is a lesson worth learning. Possessed of that wisdom, Mrs. Quin at her death can lie down as if to pleasant dreams. If she gains consolation from her Books of Hours, especially the *Hours* of Robert Bonnefoy, it is not stated explicitly; Cecily imagines that Mrs. Quin does and respects the privacy of the imagined devotions. And who is to say that Mrs. Quin, supported in the lonely nights by both knowledge and Book, did not find healing at last for all the losses of her life?

At one time, however, her isolation has been broken. Her son's daughter Tracy was sent to stay with her when the parents were divorced; and there at China Court the little girl absorbed the *mystique* of the house, its history and its customs, like the ceremony of making tea. Later the child went back to America to live with her mother, but Tracy and her grandmother had made a permanent connection. Years afterward, Tracy arrives at China Court on the night following her grandmother's death. When the old lady's will is opened, Tracy finds that Mrs. Quin has left China Court to her—slighting the four daughters in favor of a granddaughter. There are two conditions: first, that Tracy marry Peter St. Omer, the tenant of Penbarrow, the family farm; and second, that they live at China Court. Instinctively, Mrs. Quin has foreseen that the two young people, although they have never met, will make good mates; and she knows from their characters that they will love and respect the old house as her daughters do not. After these coincidences and contrivances, it comes as no surprise that Tracy and Peter do accept the conditions, that they do marry and live—not always happily, perhaps, but as well as two persons may—ever after at China Court.

So much for the romantic? But no. Hardly has the practical question arisen—How can two penniless young people maintain an old manor house?—when the means is provided for them to do so. Not even Mrs. Quin, with all her prescience, could foresee the problem or contrive a solution. But the old books, the first and rare editions that great-grandaunt Eliza had preserved or bought sixty years before, are right where she left them: in dusty paper wrappers, filling old bookcases that the unliterary Quins have scarcely ever touched. And it is soon discovered that the hoard is extremely valuable, some of the volumes (including the Bonnefoy *Hours*) worth several thousand pounds apiece. To the dismay of Tracy's aunts, the books all belong to her, along with the other contents of the house. Now China Court is able to provide for its own, in order that its own may provide for the house. The books will be sold, and China Court can remain in the family to be loved and treasured as the years pass, and to store up memories of its own for generations to come: "The stories are all different . . . yet they are all alike in that, as with every day, they must be lived through from sunrise to sunset, all the hours of the day; and as the day ends, it begins,' says Mrs. Quin."[21] And thus the two novels bordering on fantasy—*Take Three Tenses* and *China Court*—like their predecessor, *The Lady and the Unicorn,* may be seen as developments of the same theme: the vast and inexorable sweep of time. And that is also the theme of Rumer Godden's masterpiece among her shorter works.

III   The River

The River (1946) is a masterpiece because it is Rumer Godden's most compact, most effective expression of her most enduring themes: the vulnerability of childhood, the pangs of adolescence, the discovery of evil, and the consequent loss of innocence—and thence the discovery of the irreversible flow of time. This novel contains her most effective expression of this theme because its few symbols (the River, the Garden, the Snake) are intensely realized yet entirely natural in context; because the brief narrative moves surely and swiftly to its inevitable conclusion, which is that experience has no conclusion but death; and because in the telling she has stripped away all sentimentality (though not all sentiment), all romantic paraphernalia, all extraneous personage and incident, leaving her reader to feel that Rumer Godden, not Euclid alone, has looked on beauty bare.

The narrative of *The River* is of the simplest kind. A family of English children—three girls and a boy—are growing up in a Bengali river town (much as Rumer Godden and her three sisters did); their father is in charge of a jute-pressing works. Bea is the oldest; Harriet, the protagonist, called Harry, is next; then there is Bogey, their brother, a secret and silent boy who, though he lives with the family, lives apart; and last is Victoria, little more than a baby. The point of view is almost entirely Harriet's; the reader scarcely sees her father; and her mother is hardly more prominent than Nan, the children's Anglo-Indian nurse.

The older girls have not been sent home to England for schooling (as Miss Godden was) because it is wartime, but the girls do not find their education slighted. In the earliest pages, Harriet and Bea are beginning to see (though they do not yet know) how all human experiences are linked together. They are at home because there is a real war; and Harriet's first Latin declension is of war—*Bellum, Bellum, Bellum, Belli, Bello, Bello*—and her first conjugation is of love—*Amo, Amas, Amat, Amamus, Amatis, Amant*. They read *Antony and Cleopatra*—on the twin themes of war and love. They receive from their mother an embarrassing lecture on the facts of life and love, for Bea is already suffering the pangs of puberty and Harriet is approaching that age.

Love and life, war and death—they begin to seem inescapable. When Harriet asks what is troubling Bea, "She is growing up," Nan answers. "We all have to, willy-nilly."[22] Whether they will or not, people are born, grow up, and die. Death has not yet entered Harriet's little world, but there are signposts all around her, troubling signs of death that as yet she does not fully recognize. One of these signs is Captain John, a young man terribly wounded in the war, who has come maimed and lonely to work at the jute mill. Another is Bathsheba, an aged pet guinea pig, that Harriet finds one day lying stiff and stinking in its cage. That night she cannot sleep; she weeps to think that all must go like that—Mother, Nan, and all. She decides that she must really become a poet; she has written poems, and that would be a kind of immortality, she believes: to have a poem survive her.

She proves her ability as an author. She writes not a poem but a little story called "The Halo That Was Too Tight," makes Captain John type it for her, and sends it to a Calcutta paper. On Christmas morning (the only obvious contrivance in this little book) the paper and a letter arrive; the paper contains her story and the letter a check in payment. This experience Rumer Godden herself had as a child, however contrived the timing of this incident might seem; and it carries conviction. Harriet has made her mark on the world, is assured that she can and will be important to others, and is not doomed to pass utterly from out of life.

Still another sign of ever-present death is a kingfisher that startles Harriet one day; it has struck a fish in the water and has perched on a post "with the fish still bending and jerking in its beak. The poor fish had been placidly, happily, swimming and feeding . . . and then out of its element, from another, it had been seized and carried off." And Harriet also notices that "whatever happened, a fish's death, a wreck, storm, sun, the river [representing time, or history] assimilated it all."[23]

But there is human death as well; in the European cemetery in the town there is a gravestone commemorating one John Fox, a piper, who died at fourteen—two hundred years ago. And Harriet and Bogey, unknown to their elders, have watched the funeral pyre of an Indian woman and, hardly noticing, have seen her ashes scattered on the river. Nevertheless, despite all these signposts, the children remain for a time relatively untouched by death. That death should enter Harriet's life more directly is to be expected in a story of this kind, but that it comes in the manner it does is testimony to the taste and skill of the author. So many children in fiction have been deeply impressed by the death or funeral of a parent or grandparent that the situation is common, even trite, no matter how familiar it may be in life; but Rumer Godden has avoided that particular episode in *The River*.

Harriet's brother Bogey, and Harriet herself sometimes, have seemed like a pair of innocents in Eden. The garden around their house is very beautiful, and Bogey explores it with wonder and delight, keeping his own counsel, never reporting the stings and bites and falls that come his way. But a Serpent dwells in Eden, a type of knowledge and of death; and this cobra which lives there is seen only by the little boy himself and by the gateman, Ram Prasad. It is also known to Harriet, for Bogey tells her that he has seen it and that he puts out saucers of milk for the snake. But Harriet is still part child, she is engrossed by her own interests, and she fails even to report her knowledge.

One afternoon, when all in the family are napping, Harriet goes to find Bogey. He is not in the house, nor in the servants' quarters, nor in the stable. Finally, under the peepul tree, she comes upon a saucer of milk, upset and broken, and Bogey's whistle and hat. Nearby, Bogey himself is lying stiffly on his face, quite blue. By sunset of that day, according to the necessity of that hot land, Bogey's body is lying in a new grave in the old cemetery. The Indians have cut flowers, the Europeans have come by water and by land to call at the Big House, a coffin has been found and fitted to Bogey's body and has been carried by his father and a friend to the graveyard, and all is quickly over.

As swiftly almost as thought, Bogey has gone from them; Harriet in shock is sick for two days. Two large cobras are found and killed in the garden; Ram Prasad is dismissed; Bogey's toys are packed away, out of his mother's sight. Harriet, one night, picks up Bogey's toothbrush that has been overlooked; she tries to conceal it, but Nan tells her what she already knows: that she cannot keep the toothbrush, and that she does not need it anyway. Without such reminders Bogey is with her still, but the toothbrush can only be a painful symbol of his absence.

In spite of her knowledge, Harriet is shocked that living continues much as before. She herself is beginning again to feel occasional happiness when one day a visitor, an older girl, discovers Harriet's secret book in which she has written intimate observations of family and friends. The older girl reads parts of it aloud, taunting Harriet. Finding the members of her audience all against her, however, the visitor snaps, "I don't see why *Harriet* should be so haughty when everyone knows it was her fault Bogey died."[24]

Now the full extent of Harriet's new knowledge is clear to her. No one until now has said a word of reproach about her failure to report the cobra, though she knows her parents are aware of her fault. When the terrible charge is flung in her face, Harriet can only turn and run; she requires the help and the combined wisdom of Nan and Captain John before she can face the world again. Her new knowledge gained from them is not only of life and death, but of evil as well as good, of guilt and retribution—within herself: " 'You could have thought,' said Nan. 'You didn't use your sense. You know you didn't, and for that a cruel lesson has been given.' Her voice trembled and she looked with indescribable pity at Harriet, but she went on. 'Very cruel, but perfectly just,' said Nan. 'You can't complain about it. You must not.' "[25]

But death does not end everything, nor does guilt destroy Harriet's life. Preparations for her mother's new baby go on, and Harriet watches them with wonder. She flies a kite, assisted by Ram Prasad, now newly reinstated in his job. When she asserts her independence of his aid, he retorts that "Bogey Baba" could have done it better; and their cruel bickering becomes a part of Harriet's healing. Writing a poem, flying a kite, making a baby "complete outside and inside"—the creative acts of life, Harriet sees now, are very great, and she records her sense of its creative continuity in an unfinished poem quoted at the beginning of this chapter.

The tale of Harriet's awakening to life proceeds quite simply. No doubt all great truths are simple: certainly the events in her story are neither great nor rare. But the universality of her experience gains force from the simplicity of its narrative and from Rumer Godden's quiet, wise, and humorous touch. Nevertheless, the story is somewhat more complex than a reader may perceive at first glance. The River, the Garden, the Tree, and the Snake are familiar symbols, but some others are not so ob-

Crispian Woodgate

RUMER GODDEN

TWAYNE PUBLISHERS, INC.
31 UNION SQUARE WEST   NEW YORK, N. Y. 10003

vious. There is, for instance, the puff-wait-puff sound of the steam press at the jute works; the press is a pulse in the lives of the persons within its sound. Like a giant clock, it ticks the passing of each moment, and the passing has its parallel in the current of the river nearby.

Moreover, Harriet has a good-luck charm that she does not understand. Captain John and Nan one day helped the children tell fortunes by dropping bits of lead foil into hot water, then dipping them out to cool. Each bit assumed a different shape representative of its owner's future. Harriet's was a ball marked rather like a globe: "I have it still," she says at the very end of her story, "but I never found out what it meant." It meant, evidently, the world; however inscrutable, the world is all before her, at any rate. Bogey's charm, significantly, refused on that day to take any shape at all; he picked it up, rolled it into a ball, and played marbles with it.

Gently, without surprises, except for death which is always surprising to those who live, Rumer Godden has told in *The River* a wise and beautifully true story. Like most of her longer novels, it lays stress upon the continuity of life, the eternality of experience, the immortality of events. Unlike some of the others, it does so briefly and simply.

CHAPTER 5

Children Adrift

F OR young Harriet in *The River*, time in its swift onrushing brings with it both healing and new powers. Although, in a sense, this theme underlies most of Rumer Godden's fictions, it is nowhere more poignantly stated than in her stories treating children or young persons who, unlike Harriet, are cut off from the normal security of home and loving parents. Initially, perhaps, the abandoned-child motif in such stories as "The Little Fishes," "Down Under the Thames," and "The Little Black Ram," especially where these stories are somewhat autobiographical, may seem false or contrived to some degree, for Miss Godden appears to have stacked the weight of circumstance against these children.

One wonders if she is asking pity, by means of these fictitious children, for her own similar sufferings; the question is a natural one, but the answer must be negative. By good fortune and by exerting some strength, these children manage to survive their ordeals as Miss Godden did hers; indeed, they even triumph in the sense that they grow during the process. Much as it may hurt at the time, severing the cords to childhood is unavoidable on the way to maturity. What is true of the protagonists of these stories, moreover, is true of certain children in the novels as well: Lark Ingoldsby of *Take Three Tenses*, Teresa of *Kingfishers Catch Fire*, Lovejoy Mason of *An Episode of Sparrows*, the Bullock children of *The Greengage Summer*, Hugh and Caddie of *The Battle of the Villa Fiorita*, and Kizzie of *The Diddakoi*. If the Lemarchant sisters of *The Lady and the Unicorn* do not also triumph, the fault may be laid at Rumer Godden's door; for, from the first paragraph of that deterministic novel, the girls are bound to fail.

I. *Four Stories*

he peculiar poignance of this abandoned-child motif may well derive from the author's own sense of having been abandoned when she and a sister were sent away from their parents, first to their grandmother's London house and later to a succession of English schools.[1] It is pointless to object that Jon and Rumer Godden were economically and socially secure middle-class children surrounded by relatives and others concerned with their welfare. The point is that they did not *feel* secure, that the arrangements made by their elders for their benefit were precisely the circumstances that gave the girls their sense of rejection by their parents. The experience of rejection, whether real or imagined, is a quite frequent phenomenon in real life and a frequent subject for Rumer Godden's treatment in fiction.

Jon and Rumer Godden are reflected in Deborah and Alice, in "Down Under the Thames," two small girls who also have left India to live with their grandmother and aunts in London. On a November evening in 1913, Deborah asks nurse McCann to go to the bathroom with Alice (who, like the real-life Rumer, was five years old that year); "She's frightened of the seat. In India she had a little wicker chair—" Indeed, it is a fearsome thing: "The lavatory had an immense mahogany seat that stretched from wall to wall, and a pan of willow-pattern china, so wide and so frighteningly deep that it was enough to drown a small Alice in; worse, there was a brass handle in the seat that pulled up and released a terrifying cascade of water, enough to wash her away. 'Where would I go?' she asked fearfully." And Deborah answers:

"Down drains and long, long tunnels into a big black pool down under the Thames. . . ."[2] McCann, however, insists that Alice should not act like a baby.

But the terror of the lavatory seat is an experience that at last helps Alice directly to master her alien environment. One of their maiden aunts, a great hand with her needle, is teaching them to embroider and is driving little Alice beyond the limits of her skill and patience. When Alice's awkward "tray cloth" is finally finished, Aunt Gwenda scornfully rips out all the stitches and orders her to begin again. Alice, matching her anger with her aunt's, goes upstairs and returns; Aunt Gwenda de-

mands to know where the tray cloth is. "Alice lifted her eyes
and looked at Aunt Gwenda. 'Down under the Thames.'"[3]
Lonely and perpetually frightened she may be, but the "baby"
has found in righteous anger a mature courage and dignity.

Another small girl named Alice is the protagonist of an earlier
story which, curiously enough, also involves both needlework
and the calls of nature: the very slight sketch in *Harper's*, "You
Needed to Go Upstairs."[4] A ten-year gap in publication dates
suggests that this sketch is a preliminary and very different draft
of "Down Under the Thames." Alice and her mother are sitting
in the garden in the warm sun of an early spring day; Alice
is learning to knit, but "just when everything is comfortably
settled, you need to go upstairs."[5] Nothing really happens, except
that the child is made to feel useless and troublesome. The
story is, however, remarkable: first, because of its extreme delicacy (Alice is blind, but her blindness is never once mentioned);
second, because it is Rumer Godden's only published narrative
in the second-person point of view.

Like Deborah and Alice of "Down Under the Thames," Ruth
and Rumer Godden at "St. Monica's school" in "The Little
Fishes" are despised and rejected for their utter difference from
their schoolmates, as an earlier chapter of this study pointed
out. Yet, painful as their ordeal is, they learn from it the lesson
of survival. Sister Laura Mary's apology ("I beg your pardon. . . . No one is scum")[6] is small comfort by any standard,
but at least it acknowledges that the girls are important as indi-
viduals; just as Alice asserted herself in anger, Ruth and Rumer
have won the right to be considered as persons. Although rejection and pain are allowed to be pathetic in her stories, Miss Godden does not really ask her readers to weep sentimental tears for
her children. On the contrary, the children's own tears, like the
anger of others, are often the means and the signal of their
achieving maturity, as is the case in "The Little Black Ram";[7]
and she never insists on the pathos.

Jassoof is a young hellion who bedevils the older members
of his nomadic Moslem tribe in "The Little Black Ram." The
elders cannot decide what to do with the troublesome orphan
with the black curls, who defies authority and destroys beautiful
and useful things. At last he is put to herding sheep, a bitter
task in this tribe which regards sheep as soft and weak. Jassoof

chafes at the humiliation until one of the ewes gives birth to twin lambs, one of them a black ram. From the first, Jassoof feels an affinity for this new black sheep, which he treats with far more care than he gives to the other lambs; love is for him a new experience. As the little black ram grows into trouble-some adolescence, it, like Jassoof, is despised and derided. When the young ram's leg is broken, Jassoof expects the animal to be destroyed, so he is humbly grateful when crusty old Ezekiel splints the leg; now he is capable of admiring not only the old man's skill but also his patience and compassion.

Late in the season, the clan leader decides to move with his people and flocks. Because of his injured pet, Jassoof is put in charge of all the weaker animals, but his patience and industry are now matters for admiration among his elders. As they are struggling through a difficult mountain pass in a heavy snowfall, Jassoof labors mightily to save his straggling charges; but he is forced at last to abandon several of them, including his black ram. Having fallen far behind the tribe and its herds, Jassoof finally yields to the urging of his fellows and climbs to safety, hearing behind him the bleating of his beloved ram. On easier ground, as he runs to catch up, he is overtaken by another new feeling. For the first time he grieves for something outside himself, and all Miss Godden says about that is this: "He stood still while his tears fell fast."[8] Sentiment, yes; sentimentality, no.

II   An Episode of Sparrows

Similarly, young Lovejoy Mason of *An Episode of Sparrows* (1955) is drawn from her alienation in the midst of her fellow creatures by a concern for something outside herself. In Love-joy's case, that something is a garden—a most unusual kind of garden. Lovejoy is a ten-year-old "street sparrow." Catford Street in London, though shabby, is not a slum; but many of its residents, including Lovejoy, live marginal existences. Her mother, a singer, travels constantly; and, when Lovejoy is too old for little-child roles, she must be left behind. The Combies, who have a restaurant in Catford Street and have rented a room to Lovejoy's mother, are left with the child on their hands, for Mrs. Mason neglects to pay the rent and to send money for Lovejoy's clothing. When the mother does visit now and then, she is occupied with men callers—for whose sake Lovejoy (ironical name) is shut out of their room.

One day on the street, Lovejoy snatches a small, colorful packet from the hands of another child, who has picked it off the pavement. The packet, she discovers, contains cornflower seed. Seeds are to be planted, and where in Catford Street is there earth to spare for a garden? Thus begins a tiny epic of fortitude and courage. Lovejoy clears a small patch of ground in the rubble of a bombed-out building. She steals other seeds, and she robs the candle box in the Church of Our Lady of Sion in order to buy tools and grass seed. And then, just as her garden is sprouting, a gang of boys smashes it before her eyes; to them, she has trespassed upon their turf. The tender blades of grass, the tiny flower sprouts are beaten to earth—as Lovejoy has been kicked about and crushed in a hostile society. But in the world of Rumer Godden's imagination, street sparrows and grass blades that fall to earth may rise again.

Lovejoy rises. Her grief at the senseless destruction and her self-control in adversity strike the sixteen-year-old gang leader, Tip Malone, with strange force. Clumsily, he tries to make amends by finding her a new, safe garden spot behind the temporary structure of the Catholic church, among the ruins of the bombed church. There, watched over by a statue of the Blessed Virgin through a window in the sanctuary, the new Eden begins to take shape. Neither Adam nor Eve is entirely innocent, but Tip at least is a churchgoing boy. He teaches Lovejoy to genuflect and to say "Hail Mary," and he makes her replace the money she stole from the candle box. Because she has scarcely any means of getting the money, Tip gives her the proceeds of a part-time job. Moreover, this proud gang leader willingly completes his private humiliation by working in the garden himself—secretly. And, when the soil in the new garden is found to be too shallow, Tip helps take earth from the private Garden in nearby Mortimer Square.

From the high rear windows of her home in Mortimer Square, an earthly virgin watches godlike over the doings in Catford Street. Miss Olivia Chesney feels a kinship with the street sparrows and a yearning to be somehow fruitful. Unlike her sister Angela, who is an energetic member of committees and charitable boards, Olivia has never done anything but watch, if sympathetically. Nevertheless, before Lovejoy's story has been told, Miss Olivia gets her chance, and she acts.

Tip and Lovejoy are caught in the act of taking earth from the garden, and Miss Angela, as chairman of the garden committee, is officially concerned in the case; she is eager to punish what she considers vandalism if not positively theft. Her sister Olivia is more sensitive; and, though painfully shy, she speaks out on behalf of both young persons. When the Combies lose their restaurant and can no longer keep Lovejoy, Olivia wishes to adopt her but is prevented from trying to do so by the knowledge that she has a serious heart ailment; instead, she alters her will. Tip, meanwhile, has attracted the notice of a retired admiral who, sensing the boy's manliness and natural leadership, gets him an appointment to a navy training ship—Tip's heart's desire. Lovejoy, on the other hand, must go into the Anglican House of Compassion, which is hateful to her. She is even forbidden to say goodbye to Tip, whose mother holds her responsible for his public disgrace as a vandal. Her own mother has disappeared, the Combies must move away soon, and now Mrs. Malone rudely shuts the door in her face. Lovejoy knows the dull anguish of alienation: "Lovejoy had thought she knew what it was like to be alone when she was lost, alone lying waiting for her mother in bed, and sitting on the stairs while the gentlemen were in the room; she had learned to manage without her mother . . . but there had always been someone—Vincent, Mrs. Combie, then Tip."[9] Now she is utterly alone.

And now, conveniently, Miss Olivia Chesney dies, she of the truly compassionate spirit. Her revised will fulfills everybody's needs. It provides for the establishment of a trust "to open a restaurant in the West End . . . to be managed by Mr. Combie . . . on condition that he and his wife provide a home for Lovejoy Mason, treating her . . . as if she were their own child. . . . Vincent [Mr. Combie] is to be given a half share after five years; the other half is to be divided between the boy Tip Malone and Lovejoy Mason."[10]

A few years after the publication of *An Episode of Sparrows,* Miss Godden paid high tribute to a story she had read as a child: a book significantly entitled *The Secret Garden,* by Frances Hodgson Burnett. Perhaps its plot was in her mind when she wrote the book about Lovejoy Mason. "Anyone who has much to do with children knows that a naughty or disagreeable heroine is far more interesting than a good one,"[11] she remarked, apropos of little Mary who goes to live with an uncle in *The Secret Garden*.

" 'Is there anything you want?' her misanthropic Uncle Craven asks her soon after she arrives. 'Do you want toys, books, dolls?'
" 'Might I, quavered Mary, 'might I have a bit of earth?' "[12]

And Mary's garden, discovered eventually, is as troublesome and as rewarding as Lovejoy's.

III   The Greengage Summer

A whole family of children are figuratively cast adrift in *The Greengage Summer* (1959).[13] The Greys (minus the father, who is on a three-year expedition in Tibet) are traveling in Europe when mother suddenly becomes very ill and is confined to a hospital at Vieux-Moutiers in France.

That leaves Joanna ("Joss"), sixteen; Cecil, thirteen, the narrator; Hester, ten; William ("Willmouse"), seven; and Vicky, four—four girls and a small boy—to fend for themselves in a strange French town without money or friends or even much knowledge of the language. They might have had a great deal of difficulty under such circumstances, but there is in the Hôtel des Oeillets where they are staying a dashing young Englishman named Eliot, who smooths the way for them.

Although Eliot seems kind and sufficiently sophisticated to anticipate most of their needs, he cannot always be present, and at this time the children particularly need Mrs. Grey. Cecil, the narrator, is an especially sensitive girl; and in that hot August in France, she is becoming a woman. Nor would any mother, even the unconventional Mrs. Grey, knowingly choose Eliot as the mentor for her young daughter, for that suave Englishman is evidently having an affair with Mademoiselle Zizi, the hotel owner; more frightening still, he leads a mysterious double life, visiting Paris at odd times and driving a big Rolls-Royce without doing anything to suggest how he comes by his money.

The children do not come through the summer unscathed. Each child is in some way altered by the experience, for a loss of innocence (that phrase became the title of the Columbia film) is always just that, a loss; wisdom, even a knowledge of evil, is acquired at a terrible cost. Not only the souls of the little Greys but also their lives are endangered, for *The Greengage Summer* is also a mystery story, and the melodramatic ending includes a murder and a daring escape. Nevertheless, it *is* a greengage summer for the Grey offspring, a rich time of warmth and growth and, for the older girls, of ripening. The plums referred to in the title are ripe in that August, and the children fill themselves with the fruit—again, as in Lovejoy's garden and in Harriet's, symbolic fruit: the knowledge of good and of evil.

IV Breakfast with the Nikolides

Young Emily Pool and her small sister Binnie in *Breakfast with the Nikolides* (1942) are not physically separated from their mother Louise; but Emily and Louise are invariably antagonistic; and, during the eight years of Louise's separation from Charles Pool, Emily has felt her isolation severely. Now, in the little East Bengal town of Amorra, the family is reunited, but the hostility between mother and daughter does not decline; it increases. When Emily begins to mature in body, Louise admits confusedly to herself that she resents her daughter's individuality, perhaps is jealous of her as a woman: "It's the country . . . I hate it. Look what it has done to Emily. I don't want her to grow up. She is still a child. She shall be a child. . . . Emily, stop. . . . I will give in to you forever if only you will stop it; if only you will take that look off your face, try and be more natural and childish. . . . I did kill Don [Emily's spaniel]. You guessed it and you were right. I did lie to you. . . . I was caught in it even before it was done and that [your growing up] is why I did it. . . ."[14]

When Louise runs to Emily's room to make peace, the girl's bed is empty. Besides, it is too late; Emily is no longer a child. In sending her to visit a neighboring Greek family while the dog was being put down secretly, Louise herself has hastened the girl's maturation; for Emily has already reflected: "I have turned old. . . . Something left off being in me then. I put on my clean clothes . . . and I went out to breakfast. . . . I shall never go blind like that again. I shall never be blind. . . . And even to so young a girl as Emily there was something pitiable in the loss of that heedlessness. Breakfast with the Nikolides was always to be the last hour of her childhood."[15]

Through grave difficulties of several kinds, Emily has shaken off her bonds to her parents. She is free in spirit. At the end of the novel—and at the end of Diwali, the Hindu Feast of Lights—Emily lights a tiny lamp in a *puja* offering which she sets afloat on the water of a pool. Emily Pool is no longer merely adrift; she is an entity, an offering in herself, floating purposefully and shedding an independent light.

V   The Battle of the Villa Fiorita

Emily Pool was too small, when Charles and Louise separated, to know what misery was in store for her as a result; but Hugh and Caddie Clavering of *The Battle of the Villa Fiorita* (1963) are fourteen and eleven when their parents are divorced—old enough to resent the injury to themselves and young enough to wish their mother back no matter what the cost, but too young to know, as their older sister Philippa does, that a woman's life is considered to be her own. In the eyes of adults, an unfaithful wife may be reprehensible in leaving her children as well as her husband, but she is allowed to do so. In the eyes of her children, however, Fanny Clavering has betrayed them, and they feel justified in taking any measures to restore their mother to her family—and themselves to their former comfort and security.

What they do is to follow Fanny to Italy, where she occupies a lakeside villa with Rob Quillet, her film-director lover, whom she expects to marry. Using money from the sale of Caddie's beloved pony, Topaz, they make their way to the Villa Fiorita, where they intrude upon the privacy of the lovers. They are joined by Quillet's ten-year-old daughter in a series of intrigues, culminating in a hunger strike, that are directed against the union of the two lovers. But, when the children have won at last, when Quillet and his daughter have left the villa, and when Fanny, acknowledging defeat, is willing to return to England, their victory is to Hugh a hollow one. Caddie has found the grace to pity her mother's despair, but she can only be glad to have won, to know that her family will be whole again. Hugh, however, who has grown more, understands his contradictory feelings for his mother and the attractions that girls have lately held for him; and he has grown to love Rob's daughter Pia, whom he saved from drowning after they had foolishly gone sailing in rough weather. Rob Quillet has been driven away—good; but Pia has gone with her father, and Hugh wonders if he will ever see her again. He has become a man within, man enough to understand that there is no real pleasure without pain, no lasting victory without some taste of defeat: "This was the juggernaut power of adults, crushing what they did not even see, and for the first time Hugh was close to tears . . . he remembered that [Pia] would be living with her grandmother, the Nonna she talked about, and he did not know even Nonna's name. Write to Rob? . . . but he could not write to Rob. Ask Fanny. . . ? Hugh knew he could never ask her now."[16]

Nowhere in Miss Godden's stories is the war between the generations depicted so startlingly. The children have not waged their battle at the Villa Fiorita for the sanctity of marriage but for the inviolability of the mother-child relation. Rumer Godden indicates in this novel that a mother's life is not her own until her children have been reared.

Romance, even romantic fantasy, has an important place in life, but the end of the novel suggests symbolically that romance must not be allowed to disguise the anguish of real experience: "As the car drove out of the gates, Caddie noticed what she had not seen before; that the whitethorn flowers had dropped, their petals were scattered in the road. The hedges now did not disguise their pricks and, almost before the car turned up the road, Giulietta ran and shut the gates. The last thing Hugh and Caddie saw were the gilt letters [on the gates], VILLA FIORITA, as, with Fanny sitting between them, they drove away."[17] The petals of Fanny's romance are scattered in the dust, the thorns of life are laid bare, and the gates of her "Flower Villa" are shut to her forever.

VI   The Diddakoi

Miss Godden's recent "novel" for children, *The Diddakoi,*[18] is yet another exercise upon the abandoned-child theme; and although the now familiar recipe is stirred up with fresh spices, nevertheless the ingredients are recognizable as having been measured out from other shelves in the Godden pantry. Little

Kezia, or Kizzie, is a half-breed orphan living with her Gypsy
great-great-grandmother in a caravan in Sussex. Gypsy life and
customs were first treated by Miss Godden in *Gypsy, Gypsy*
(1940); and the old woman, in her remoteness from her small
descendant Kizzie, resembles the elderly lady glimpsed in the
juvenile story *The Fairy Doll* (1956)—the old lady whose great-
granddaughter Elizabeth "was always being left out or made
to stay behind."[19]

When Kizzie's aged relative dies, the little girl is left alone,
like Lovejoy Mason of *An Episode of Sparrows* (and like Lark,
Teresa, the Bullock children, and Hugh and Caddie, in four
other novels preceding *The Diddakoi*), but is taken in by adults
whose intended kindness she suspects and resists. Like Teresa
and Moo of *Kingfishers Catch Fire*, Kizzie is spitefully attacked
by village children of an alien race; but like Lovejoy Mason
(and like Jassoof of "The Little Black Ram" and Emily Pool
of *Breakfast with the Nikolides*), Kizzie has resources of hard-
ness, resilience, and intelligence that enable her to survive. And
when a *deus ex machina* resolution apparently grants Kizzie
a long and happy life to come, Godden readers will recognize
the device that saved the plots of *Kingfishers, China Court*,
and *In This House of Brede*.

VII *Suffer Little Children*

"Corot painted too many silver trees; and Rumer Godden describes too many brave children," Virgilia Petersen once remarked; but she went on to acknowledge that Corot trees and
Godden children, "once seen, become part of our vision for
good."[20] Moreover, each painting, like each story, is an individual
work of art; it lives or dies chiefly according to its own merits.
Of course, a particular work may gain a certain longevity if
it also illuminates an artist, or a period, or a culture; but, because
such illumination is secondary to the act of creation, it is begging
the question to dismiss a work (as Miss Godden's critics sometimes have done) because it does not appear to shed its light
on something else.

If Miss Godden has treated the subject of deserted children
rather frequently, it is well to remember that limitations of subject have often been a virtue in a writer who knows his subject
intimately; and it is so with her. What does it matter that Proust

plumbed the depths of his psyche too often, that Faulkner plowed and replowed the same patch of Mississippi earth, that Hemingway's he-man was worn threadbare, that Jane Austen never left the rectory, or that Dickens vindicated his unhappy childhood in novel after novel? What matters is that each novelist was chosen by his subject, not the subject by him, and that, within his limitations, he wrote what he had to write in a way unlike anyone else. What matters above all is that Rumer Godden, after long struggling, found a stance in the world—a message that touches the hearts of countless readers, and a voice so distinctively her own that few authors writing after her could treat the same subjects without being suspected of owing her a debt. Such is the service Rumer Godden has done for her fictional children.

"Every child has the right to bother me," Father Rossi tells Rob Quillet, and that Christian paraphrase may be taken as a Rumer Godden motto; she says to her reader, "Every child has the right to bother you." Taken all together, the stories and novels treated in this chapter (along with *The Lady and the Unicorn* and *Kingfishers Catch Fire*) no doubt will seem to protest too much on behalf of children in trouble everywhere. But as Miss Godden has remarked, "anyone who is truthful cannot be sentimental."[21] On its own terms, each individual work mentioned here avoids sentimentality and reminds its audience that children are no less sensitive and suffering persons than adults are; that gritty truths may lie beneath the most shimmering fantasy; and that for children of all ages some touch of fantasy may be needed to balance every degree of unpleasantness, if equanimity and sanity are to be maintained.

CHAPTER 6

Artifice and Romance

A T the age of eight, Rumer Godden wrote her life story—in fiction, so as not to be bothered by actuality. This facility at storytelling was both an inherited and an acquired gift. Her parents were inveterate storytellers, and both Jon and Rumer delighted in gruesome games of make-believe called "Iurki" that sent their juvenile guests away in fear and their mothers away in anger from tea with the Goddens in Narayangunj.[1] Not only this narrative facility has remained with Miss Godden, but also an ambivalent attitude toward her readers, one much like that toward her childish and captive audiences in India long ago. This attitude may be said to mingle charm and contempt. On the one hand, she desires and needs an appreciative audience, which her charm readily secures; on the other, she so easily captivates that audience, and its members have accepted so docilely whatever she produces, that she has been too willing to publish books and stories that depend upon stereotypes for characters and situations and upon contrivance and coincidence for plot resolutions. In some respects, she has seldom achieved the art that conceals art— that leads a viewer to step across the picture frame and immerse himself in the life depicted.

This is not to say that artifice per se diminishes the worth of any form of fiction. The fairy tale, the murder mystery, and the ghost story are respectable literary types with conventions of their own—conventions that not only employ but demand and even systematize the use of improbability and of patently artificial devices. In that sense, it is possible to make a good case for *Chinese Puzzle* and *Gypsy, Gypsy* as fairy tales; for *The Greengage Summer* as melodrama or murder mystery; for the conclusion of *Kingfishers Catch Fire* as suspense story; for parts of *The Lady and the Unicorn* and *Take Three Tenses* as ghost stories; or for *A Breath of Air* as romantic comedy in the vein of Shakespeare's *The Tempest,* of which it is a deliberate imitation.

This approach, however, is not entirely satisfactory for at least three reasons. First, none of these books fully observes the conventions of the literary type to which it has arbitrarily been assigned. Second, each one mingles its improbability quite incongruously with the most grimly realistic details. Third, their author and her publishers have offered these books to the public as novels, and as such they have been accepted by readers and reviewers. Moreover, some mingling of realistic and fantastic materials occurs in nearly all of Rumer Godden's novels and in nearly all of her books for children and young people; thus it becomes a question of degree of improbability rather than one merely of distinguishing between obviously different types of books.

The plain fact is that the novel has developed mainly out of a recent and Realistic rather than an older, Romantic tradition; so much so, in fact, that it is common to speak of the *romance* as something quite different in impulse and execution from the novel. This tendency has led Miss Godden's contemporary Graham Greene, for example, to label his book-length fictions either novels or "entertainments." But the necessity or utility of such a distinction has not apparently occurred to Miss Godden. From first to last, improbability has been allowed to color some part of each "adult" book; and, when she has found a device that appeals to her, she has not hesitated to employ it again and again, as some examples will demonstrate.

I *The God from a Machine*

In ancient Greek drama, when a playwright had involved his characters in impossible difficulties, it sometimes happened that he would provide an arbitrary, unlooked-for solution to the problems—a solution he imposed from without instead of allowing to grow naturally from within the circumstances already established. Thus the plot resolution might involve a crane or pulley arrangement by means of which a god would be lowered to the stage to set things right among the humans—literally, *deus ex machina,* the god from a machine.

Because such facile contrivances or coincidences are not infre-

quent among beginning writers of fiction as well as drama, it
is not surprising that Rumer Godden, in her first novels, should
have employed just such a device. What astonishes is that the
very latest novels often employ *deus ex machina* in less acceptable ways than her first books did, almost as if she has
grown contemptuous of her readers' judgment. For example,
there is a device that may be called the "hidden-treasure discovery" in *In This House of Brede, China Court,* and *The Lady
and the Unicorn*—and in all three books the discovered treasure
offers an alternative to the destruction of an old house and the
dispersion of a family. *Brede* portrays a house of Benedictine
nuns whose monastery is in great need of repairs, for which
they have no money. Someone accidentally breaks a scapular
cross that has long been valued for its association with their
order, and finds inside a large ruby, the sale of which will provide the money needed for repairs. In *China Court,* as has been
discussed, an old lady dies, willing her beloved house to a granddaughter rather than to one of her four daughters, in the confident faith that the granddaughter will love and maintain it
as its mistress has done. Mrs. Quin has no way of knowing
how Tracy can provide the means, nor does Tracy herself until
she discovers that a former resident of the house, unknown to
the owners, filled its bookshelves with rare volumes and first
editions, the sale of which will provide the money now needed
for maintaining the house.

Rare books are not related to anything of the present day
in *China Court,* except that Mrs. Quin has kept a lovely old
Book of Hours at her bedside; and jewels as such have nothing
to do with the plot or the characters or the setting of *In This
House of Brede.* Yet in a much earlier novel than these, Rumer
Godden employed a similar device almost carelessly but to far
greater effect. In *The Lady and the Unicorn,* as in these two
later books, an old house is in danger of being destroyed because
no one in the present generation perceives its worth. The
Lemarchant house is at last torn down, however, and the sorry
remnants of the old family it once sheltered are scattered and
humiliated. The youngest daughter of the family hopelessly
searches in the rubble for the marble tablet that represents what
the house and the family have once been. Instead of the tablet
she finds a sundial, now split and toppled, that had once stood

in the garden. As Blanche idly examines the split dial, she finds a row of tiny stones once concealed and now revealed; she rubs one of them until it sparkles—a gem stone, though she does not know it. Suddenly she hears a noise; to escape being discovered where she is forbidden to play, she runs away, dropping the stone, ironically, and leaving behind all the treasure that some ancestor provided for just such dire predicaments as hers.

In other words, a device that might have provided the usual happy ending for a story alternately sordid and romantic is here employed for an opposite effect: to show that romance is shattered by harsh reality, that suffering is the human condition, and that much potential good is lost in the destruction of even the humblest human creature. Although the dirt-encrusted gems in the sundial are not very subtle symbols for the wretched descendants of the once-wealthy Lemarchants, nevertheless as lost wealth they have an organic relation to the theme and plot; and they serve to deepen the difficulties and the sense of loss, not to relieve them arbitrarily, as happens in the two later novels.

Another way of looking at too-facile plot resolutions is provided by two other novels, in which the appearance of a human character effects such a swift change in the situation that he might as well have been costumed as a god and lowered by a pulley to the stage. The impulsive Sophie Barrington Ward of *Kingfishers* and her daughter Teresa have arrived at a crisis in their lives—Teresa, gravely injured; Sophie, in some danger of her life in a hostile, alien place—when an old friend and former suitor arrives from England just in the nick of time: Dr. Toby, stepping from an automobile into Sophie's situation, almost literally *deus ex machina*. It is quite unexpected, totally unprepared for: Toby has scarcely been mentioned earlier, except in a sort of prologue that is set in a time after the main action; and Teresa's message that summoned him has been kept secret not only from her mother but from the reader as well.

Kingfishers, an engrossing and compelling novel, is flawed at the end by this gratuitous contrivance. Yet, when the same device is used in another and weaker novel, *The Greengage Summer,* it creates not a ripple of disbelief, mainly because, in the context of romantic adventure already well established, it simply does not intrude. Mr. Bullock arrives from England to take charge of his sister, who is seriously ill, and her four children, who have become involved in a murder and in other criminal activities. Like Dr. Toby, Mr. Bullock has received a summons that is kept a secret from the reader, as well as from the other characters; but, unlike Toby, Bullock has been referred to repeatedly as the children's Uncle William who might or might not be interested in helping them.

The artifice of a character's arriving just in time to prevent disaster can be either acceptable or unacceptable, without regard to whether the story as a whole is good or poor. The acceptance of the device depends on the reader's not being kept wholly ignorant but upon his being allowed to say, "Yes, I might have known that would happen." A reader who is completely hood-winked by a "butler-did-it" resolution feels cheated, as any dev-otee of detective fiction knows; but the same reader may relish being surprised if he is allowed to consider the butler as among the suspects prior to the final revelation. In much the same way, the artifice of solving everybody's problems by letting a char-acter conveniently die and leave his fortune to those who need it can seem either true or false, depending on the skill with which the novelist can manage to foreshadow the death and to make it both sensibly sad and appropriately happy as a solution. Miss Godden has frequently skirted the dangers presented by the use of this artifice. Mrs. Quin's death is the very first event in *China Court*, and the manner of her last days is later represented in many flashbacks. Although she is sympathetic as a character, the reader never has a chance to feel a loss in her death, so that her granddaughter Tracy's inheritance seems entirely happy; and, if any artifice is intrusive in that novel, it is the trove of rare books that Tracy discovers in the house.

Similarly, in *Take Three Tenses* old General Dane's life is plainly over long before his death—he is unwillingly retired and living alone with his memories of love. A brief rejuvenation occurs when he meets his grandniece Grizel, but it only inspires him to purchase the house his family has occupied under lease for a century—and to tell Grizel and her husband-to-be that the house will be theirs. Thus, when a bombing raid that same evening smashes one wall and kills the General, it is a pleasing resolution because several "flash-forwards" have told us that Grizel and Pax will marry and that their children will live hap-pily in this house.

The coincidences of arrivals and departures, of the first century's being symbolized in the General's violent death, these partially unpleasant details are lost in the startling shifts backward and forward in time and in the unconventional shifts in verb tenses. But in *An Episode of Sparrows,* when Olivia Chesney's will abruptly solves all the problems of all the characters, including some who never knew of her existence, the heavy hand of the novelist can only seem intrusive.

II *Stereotyped Character and Situation*

Olivia's will establishes a trust that provides the Combies with a restaurant to manage, Lovejoy Mason with a home, and both Lovejoy and her friend Tip Malone with a future income. It is a truly astonishing and richly satisfying conclusion—not indeed for a novel but for a fable, a fantasy, or a fairy tale. For, although many painful and ugly details of real life are faithfully depicted, *An Episode of Sparrows* bears essentially no resemblance to the carefully worked-out probabilities and the shifting, growing characters that readers have come to expect in a serious novel. Miss Godden's characters are, except for Lovejoy, mere stereotypes, and her plot resolutions are frankly contrived. Miss Angela Chesney is the Heartless Rich Woman; her sister Olivia, the Fairy Godmother; Tip Malone, the Tough Boy with a Heart of Gold. And the plot finally runs down when the (formerly) Bad Children have reformed and been rewarded, and when the Heartless Villains are properly punished.

If *Sparrows* resembles one of Miss Godden's stories for children, that is no coincidence; for, like those stories, this fantasy bears a close similarity to those of Hans Christian Andersen and Beatrix Potter, whose tales she acknowledges as models for her own works for young people. It is as if she has never lost the need for a touch of fantasy in her own emotional life; fortunately for her, millions of her readers seem to share that need.

Like the contrived plot resolution, the contrived character and the contrived situation have often been employed to produce a stock response in the reader, and Miss Godden has not flinched from stereotypes. Indeed, in one novel at least she seemed to delight in creating a monster; for, if Olivia Chesney was the Fairy Godmother of *An Episode of Sparrows,* Madame Barbe de Longuemare is the Wicked Witch of *Gypsy, Gypsy,* the novel of Rumer Godden's which, in its sharp contrasts between good and evil, innocence and depravity, most closely resembles the fairy tale. Barbe, who envies her niece Henrietta her youth and freshness, longs in some obscure way to refresh herself by despoiling the innocence of others. Her niece is not corrupted by her, however; Barbe chooses as her victim a Gypsy camping on her estate. Carefully she undermines the man's independence and the wild freedom of his children, making him greedy and corrupt. As a direct result, the Gypsy is sentenced to fifteen years' imprisonment, a punishment that totally negates his former free state and may well destroy the man as well as his spirit. So unmotivated is Barbe's cruelty that she is less a woman than a stock figure from romance or fairy tale. Rather like the old witch in *Hansel and Gretel,* she hungers for the flesh or substance of innocents, not for want of other food but from sheer malignity. More witch than woman, Barbe is a possessed body harboring an evil spirit. Entertaining her story may be, but convincing in human terms it is not and cannot be.

A similar fairy-tale air hangs over *A Candle for St. Jude.* Although the character of young Hilda French is not idealized, and although her acts are presented with as much coolness as those of Rosa Lemarchant in *The Lady and the Unicorn,* Hilda succeeds, nevertheless, as a dancer much as the standard Determined Heroine of a child's book succeeds. All obstacles fall before her single-minded assault; age, experience, and cynicism are blunted against the armor of her hope and her ego.

Finally, there are the stereotyped situations of a number of Godden narratives. Perhaps the most striking of these is the obvious contrast between the present and the past in the ghost-story episodes of *The Lady and the Unicorn.* In it, the bitter life of an Anglo-Indian girl in a grubby quarter of Calcutta is played off against the equally bitter but highly romanticized life of another girl who formerly lived in the same house. The present-day girl hears the barking of a little dog out of the past, sees the ghostly figure of her predecessor, and hears carriage wheels and horses' hooves where none have been for years. Fanny Clavering, the suburban housewife of *The Battle of the Villa Fiorita,* has her cake and eats it, too. She finds romance abroad for a time with an Italian film-director lover, thrilling all suburban-housewife readers with the thought of their own potential for romance; but she is brought to herself—and back to her husband and children—confirming those same readers in the feeling that, although they too might choose romance, they have chosen a nobler way for themselves.

In *A Candle, Unicorn,* and *Battle,* then, as occasionally in other books, the disappointments of real life are given poignance not by intensification or fresh perspective but by contrast with the beautiful simplicities of fairy tale. But the most fantastical of Miss Godden's novels is none of these but *A Breath of Air.* Just as Shakespeare took his plots wherever he could find them, so she has made free of his. *A Breath of Air* is drawn lock, stock, and plot from *The Tempest;* even the title is a modest acknowledgment of her debt.

III A Breath of Air

Rumer Godden's "Prospero" calls himself Van Loomis. Back home in Scotland he was surnamed Fyffe, and he was the Earl of Spey. But he has been superseded in the family shipping business by a younger brother; besides, he was more interested in study than in business. At Oxford, he has taken up sorcery; and, when he left Scotland after his wife's death, he made his residence on the "Indian Pacific" island of "Terraqueous," where his young daughter Charis ("Miranda") is brought up by native servants. These servants are as mixed a lot of stereotypes as ever filled a melting pot; how such oddities have come to inhabit the same island is not explained—though the author has done her part by suggesting that it is really an "island of the mind."[2] There is Pheasant, by her dialect an American Negro of the deep South; she is Charis's nurse and the namer or namegiver on the island—being responsible for such sobriquets as Serendipity, Webster, Resurrection, Orange Flower, Flora Annie, and Golden Treasury. Then there are Filipino, Van Loomis's "Ariel"; the half-breed Mario, his "Caliban," whose mother was a witch; and Niu, the native chief. The island produces crops as incongruous as its people: apples, wool, and cotton are grown there, evidently through "Prospero's" sorcery, or learning.

The enchanted island, although given some concreteness by the author's specification of longitude and latitude (123.15 E and 11.40 S), is thus stranger than fiction. There is no shipwreck

caused by a storm whipped up by the master magician, but
"Ferdinand" does arrive mysteriously, for his seaplane is forced
down by engine trouble after an unforeseen storm. His name
in the American version of this tale is Valentine—suitably romantic (although Miss Godden had first called him Kenelm,
and her English publisher concurred).[3] Valentine is accompanied
by a mechanic named McGinty who, like the shipwrecked sailors
in *The Tempest,* intrudes a gross, material reality upon the delicate island atmosphere. McGinty is given the most vulgar speech
in all Godden fictions, for his conversation spatters curses and
obscenities all about him. Some of his four-letter words, being
peculiarly British, baffle American readers.[4] At the time of this
book's appearance, it was unusual for obscenities to be publicly
distributed; but, of course, that practice has since changed.

Such Naturalistic details do not destroy the poetry of Shakespeare's play, nor do they spoil the romance of *A Breath of
Air.* It is a question, however, whether McGinty is really necessary, whether his obtrusive language serves even as a comic
relief, such as Shakespeare provides in Trinculo and Stephano.
After all, both the Godden novel and the Shakespeare play deal
with reconciliation at several levels—ultimately, reconciliation
between the worlds of magic and real life—and surely it
demeans the pain that humans suffer to represent it chiefly in
speech so gross and mindless. If McGinty and Van Loomis are
intended to represent extremes of brutality and spirituality, Mc-
Ginty takes it out in talk, and Van Loomis is neither poet nor
prophet; his contrast with McGinty is finally no more than a
difference in taste and breeding. Van Loomis does not even
think he is a magician; his powers, as far as he knows, lie in
the superstitious minds of the islanders: "'I am more conjured
against than conjuring,' Mr. Van Loomis might have said. . . ."[5]

Charis, the daughter of Van Loomis, is as naïve as Miranda;
until Valentine drops out of the sky, she has never seen a man
of her own age and race. Valentine, a well-known playwright,
is dazzlingly handsome and sophisticated. The result of their
meeting, especially under these circumstances, is utterly pre-
dictable; and it does not require a "Prospero" to lay artificial
barriers between them to insure that they should fall in love.

What the novel comes to at last is a fairy tale in modern
dress, not unlike a musical comedy, decked out in Shakespearean

parallels. It teaches no profound truths, unless it be that love will find a way, or that a hermit's life (no matter how desirable) is a practical and moral impossibility; what it does convey is that people welcome a breath of air, a release from stale custom, a veil of illusion to drop for a few moments across everyday routine. The success of the novel itself demonstrates the validity of that message.

Now it is apparent that such release must be the object Rumer Godden sought not only in *A Breath of Air* but also in *Chinese Puzzle, The Lady and the Unicorn, Take Three Tenses, China Court, Gypsy, Gypsy, A Candle for St. Jude,* and *An Episode of Sparrows.* But these and her other novels show that the real world triumphs at last. Indeed, reality must win for the sake of sanity; but illusion is the stuff that spirit feeds on. Nowhere in her works has Miss Godden stated such views more plainly than in her reverent biography of Hans Christian Andersen. Although he was incongruously homely and vain, although he made a fool of himself for great ladies like Jenny Lind, and although his plays and novels are poor things, Andersen had, nevertheless, a godlike creative and inspiring power in the medium of the tale.

IV *A Tale Which Holdeth Children*

Here, it may be, is an essential key to understanding Rumer Godden's repeated reliance on contrivance and on the perpetual charm of romance: she has not distinguished very much between her novels for adults and her stories for children. Both seem to be derived from the same impulses and to be founded on the same theory of fiction. The general principles of that theory have been stated in various places but are perhaps best summarized by Miss Godden in an essay, "The Writer Must Become as a Child," published in the same year as *Hans Christian Andersen.* Denying the common assumption that children's books are simple and easy to write, Miss Godden (at that time the author of three published juvenile books) declared that writing for children requires humility. Pointing to the authors of famous books for children, she noted that true children's classics never have a "big plot written down, but a little one written up." They must "sound well" to a child's ear; they must be dramatic, swift of movement, and clear, with "few side tracks" and "no opinions"; and, finally, they must have something more, "an aftertaste, a flavor that lingers . . . a personality."[6]

The application of these principles to her own work for children may be summarized briefly. Like Andersen, Miss Godden has avoided talking down to children; she approaches them on their level. Their interests are hers—dolls, making dollhouses and small gardens and decorated pictures, learning worldly skills and sympathy for other persons, and (not incidentally) growing up. Her language has been direct and simple but not simplified, and her characters are mostly real people, fallible and misunderstood perhaps, but well intentioned and in the end justified as they are.

But not even language and style, for which Miss Godden herself receives high marks from reviewers, can approach the importance in fiction of interesting characters truthfully treated. In fact, interesting characters may redeem an atrocious style, as she pointed out in connection with a childhood favorite of hers, *The Secret Garden,* by Frances Hodgson Burnett, author of *Little Lord Fauntleroy.* After half a century Miss Godden still remembered her first reading of *The Secret Garden.* She and her sisters in India had borrowed a copy but had to return it before they had finished reading it. Eventually, however, they received a shipment of books from England, among them a familiar green volume which they eagerly devoured. It was, she said, "chiefly a girl's book"; it was "overwritten" and its style was "dreadful"—but pompous style and improbable plot did not matter so much. What mattered was the sense of life, of interesting life at that.[7]

With this precept in mind, and before returning to the novels as such, it may be as well to examine still another expression of Rumer Godden's theory of narrative art, in the long narrative poem *In Noah's Ark.*[8] This work may be taken as representative of her verses at their best and worst. As in all her most interesting poems, animals are principal characters; and for that reason the poem foreshadows her translations from the French of *Prayers from the Ark* and *The Creatures' Choir,* by Carmen Bernos de Gasztold. *In Noah's Ark* has as its subject poetry, or poetic vision. The story of the Ark is told in highly irregular verse, irregular not only because its rhythms and rhymes are constantly shifting but also because it is composed in large part of tags and scraps and lines from poem, popular adage, biblical lore, missionary hymn, folk song, and a half dozen other literary categories.

Noah and his sons Shem, Ham, and Japheth load the animals two by two—all except one, a "horse with wings" which the literal-minded Ham wants to leave behind. Pegasus simply flies aboard, announcing, "I am poetry," and "I shall make a poet of Ham." But Ham has no time for poetry and clips his wings, or so he thinks. Pegasus, however, tells stories to the other animals (as Rumer Godden entertained her schoolmates in "The Little Fishes") and is punished as a troublemaker by being impounded. Nevertheless, his work has been done:

> a gift had fallen on the Ark,
> his gift, and the animals were speaking
> with Pentecostal tongues, telling their tales. . . .

One after another the beasts foretell their futures in myth and legend—in poetry:

> "I shall carry a conqueror," said the horse.
> "I shall nurse an empire," said the wolf.
> "I shall see a vision," said the ass.
> "I shall teach a lesson to a king," said the smug little spider.

The large dog says that, "tutored and entrusted with brandy," he should save "poor snow-blind men" (as set forth in Miss Godden's later article, "Heroic Monks of Saint Bernard");[9] and a lion "told how a saint should take a thorn out of his paw: 'and we, the lion, shall turn Christian to pay the saint the debt'" (as in her verse story, *Saint Jerome and the Lion*).[10]

The lion questions Pegasus's knowledge; and, inspired by the new sense of identity he receives from the answers, Leo vows, "I shall be good." The other animals demand of Pegasus their star-names: Hydra, Taurus, Cygnus, Pisces. But Poetry is fraught with power for evil as well as good: the animals' new sense of their own importance threatens the safety of the Ark. A duckling is found dead, stung by the scorpion who is now bragging of his status as Scorpio, and Pegasus gets the blame for that death.

Pegasus looks at his accuser and explains the nature of the
poetic gift he has brought not only to animals but to men; he
begins with a line from Henry Vaughan's "Peace":

> My soul, there is a country far beyond the stars,
> above, below, beyond, around the stars;
> the space beside the moon is it,
> the hollow of your hand is it,
> a pearl is it,
> a seed is it,
> the root and tree of life are it.

Pegasus foretells that Ham or "everyman" will follow in the
new way, traveling like Keats in realms of gold. Ham in turn
prophesies that the animals shall have their heaven on earth;
only men need a heaven elsewhere—and only men need poetry.
Of Ham's speech, Noah says wonderingly, "This is poetry."

If *In Noah's Ark* fails, as it does in part, it does so because
it does not define its audience. A poem or novel need not be
written for a given audience, of course; if it is good, it will
find its own level. But this poem (to paraphrase what its author
once said of A. A. Milne's Pooh stories) seems to have been
written partly for adults but with one eye on the children.[11]
If it succeeds, as it also does in part, *In Noah's Ark* does so
because it contains the germ of a new myth, hidden though
it be under a dozen older myths: a fresh, or at least unexpected,
way of saying that poetry is the "realms of gold." Miss Godden's
allusion to Keats was not accidental. The poetic gift releases
men from their bondage to earth or to earthly masters; it frees
them to soar among the stars, to dream great dreams, to conceive
grand hopes. Ham was already a poet when he saw that Pegasus
was "the exceptional one" in a world of beasts and bestial men.
He became exceptional himself in perceiving distinctions that
his fellows did not see—a poet, in short, in the very terms Miss
Godden has used repeatedly in defining the poet.

As for what Miss Godden's poetic and narrative theories contribute to understanding her novels, one contribution is mainly
thematic; the other, mainly technical. On the one hand, the exceptional person may be the best, because most interesting, character for fiction as well as poetry: small girls who see ghosts, old
ladies who gladly die to perform what only they can see needs

doing, even a woman so cold and cruel that she resembles a malignant spirit—these are exceptional persons, and they demonstrate the poetic gift through their being if not in their acts. On the other hand, a technique that encourages readers to dream dreams, a language and style that encourage visions, and a choice of subject matter that shows humans mostly striving upward— these are the province of the Poet, the True Writer. In Rumer Godden's terms, conventional distinctions like those between novel and romance, between poetry and fiction, are at best secondary to the real issues, which might be phrased as a question: Does it touch the heart, and speak truly of the heart?

CHAPTER 7

A Thinne Subtil Knittinge of Thinges

THE world of Rumer Godden is given life initially by her
concept of order within the flux of time, and it is given
shape by the outward forms of human experience. Then it is
fleshed out by her warm sympathy with all living creatures, especially animals and children, but tempered by a healthy skepticism
about human nature. She knows and participates in the joys and
pains of birth and death, of love and strife; but she also understands that, while people do as well as they can, their best is far
from perfect. Nevertheless, she does not preach; and, if a coherent
philosophy is to be perceived as underlying her books, stories,
poems, and articles, it may well be summarized not in her own
words but in those of Aristotle that she once quoted with ap-
proval: Happiness, she said, "can not be achieved in less than a
complete lifetime; one swallow does not make a summer, neither
does one fine day. And one day, or indeed any brief period of
felicity does not make a man happy."[1]

From this idea flows her notion of time as a stream and of
life as a continuum; and from it follows her reiterated analysis
of birth and death, of love and marriage and procreation, and
of the houses that shelter and witness those acts. For the acts
themselves are neither happy nor unhappy; rather, each is a
part of a much larger whole, composed of many such acts and
measurable only in the whole.

I Of Hearth and Home

For many years and through many books, the actions of Rumer
Godden's characters sometimes appeared less important than
the houses in which they occurred. This impression was particularly strong with *Take Three Tenses* and *China Court*, not to

mention three children's books: *The Doll's House, Mouse House,* and *Home Is the Sailor.* Each of the two novels, as Chapter 4 has indicated at length, deals with a century in the life of a family within one spacious dwelling. "In me you exist," says the house at 99 Wiltshire Place to the Dane family of *Take Three Tenses.*[2] And, although the structure named China Court does not itself speak with the sound of many voices, the novelist has included a section describing the characteristic sounds that make it a home, in a three-page apostrophe on its homeyness. For, as she says, "China Court gives off the ring of a house, a true home," much as fine porcelain rings true.[3] A lyrical, evocative, intensely nostalgic passage, it follows a section on the generations of servants and pets that have lived among the Quin family; and, since it precedes a startling confrontation at the end of a chapter, this passage on sounds, by the sheer weight of its circumstantial detail, persuades one that its author is utterly convinced of the enduring strength possessed and preserved by a solid, secure household. That mass of detail can only be suggested by brief quotation, but even in brief the catalogue itself rings true:

> The ring of home is, too, in the feel of paper, of firelight warm on fingers, of ivory piano keys and cold housekeys, in the softness of a cat's fur stroked, a child's hair brushed, in kisses, but most of all home is in sound.
> The sound of bells pealed, of clocks all over the house, from the . . . grandfather in a mahogany case, to the French clock with its painted cupid under the glass dome in the drawing room. The clocks tick and taps run. . . .[4]

There follows, after other sounds, a list of characteristic or representative speeches by former inhabitants of the house.

Take Three Tenses also has loving catalogues of the contents, physical as well as spiritual, of the old house: linens, silver, china, glass, jewelry, and so on. The wonder is that such catalogues can be acceptable parts of an essentially modern narrative, as they are in an ancient epic. The story simply has to wait while the storyteller counts the spoons, the tea sets, the sheets and pillowcases: "The house is filled with possessions like the silver strainer with the silver primrose on the handle. . . .

there is a set of spoons and forks, rat-tailed, worn fine . . . there is the new set, so much more solid, ordered from Mappin and Webb, there are toast racks and butter dishes and jam spoons; and salt-cellars and mustard-pots and a little walnut barrel capped with silver for grinding peppercorns. . . . there are all the christening mugs of course: a silver rattle and baby forks and spoons. . . ."[5] Acceptance of these passages depends, of course, on their contribution to the story. What they contribute, distinctively at least, is emotional atmosphere—the reader's recollection in tranquility of the feelings *he* associates with such possessions, together with circumstantial persuasion, under the weight of so much detail, as to the truth of the narrative. Of course they also contribute a strong characterization of the substantial middle-class occupants, and of their comfortable life.

Hugh and Caddie of *Battle* find the Villa Fiorita a storehouse of rich but appropriate furnishings; and their first, secret visit is at once a shock to them and a revelation to the reader of the solid, permanent character of the house, which is unlikely to be shaken by these mere alien transients:

It was a dining room. They noticed immediately that the tablecloth on the round table was all of lace with a branched silver candelabrum in the centre. More candlesticks were on the sideboard, a stand of pink hydrangeas in the window. There were Persian rugs in soft colors. "Well, we had Persian rugs at home," said Caddie.

"Not like these," said Hugh.

The room smelled of flowers, wine, and food. . . . Glass doors divided this room from the next, a drawing room, bare and cool, with more Persian rugs on a polished wood floor.[6]

Time and time again, in this and in other books, the author lovingly tells over the flowers, the paintings, the rugs and furniture, the silver and crystal and linens.

Passages like these understandably have great appeal for women, especially for the housewife who finds them a comforting justification of her chosen life. That is not to say, of course, that the novelist took her attitude in order to sell books; far from it. But, once having taken a valid position and found it tenable, even rewarding, she is not to be blamed for returning

to that position in story after story. For it is after all quite
clear that this nesting instinct is genuinely her own, fostered
no doubt by her unsettled early life. She once remarked, apropos
of the burning of her beloved house, Little Douce Grove, in
1963, "I think the reason family houses are so important to
me is that I have never had a settled home. Perhaps I am not
meant to."[7]

Rather like Sophie in *Kingfishers Catch Fire*, Rumer Godden
has sought to put down roots wherever she could rest for a
few months. It is not by chance that Sophie and many other
female characters share their creator's interest in making gardens. Aside from their purely esthetic appeal, gardens represent
attachment, growth, and permanence—order and a measure of
certainty and faith in the midst of constant change. It is instructive on this point to compare Sophie's career with Miss Godden's
at one stage. Her sister, the novelist Jon Godden (Mrs. Oakley),
has pointed out, in connection with *Kingfishers*, that "Dhilkusha . . . is a real house" in Kashmir and that Rumer Godden
not only lived in it but there "made a herb farm, worked in
her garden, and taught her children" in wartime, just as Sophie
does. Moreover, at a later period of her life, Rumer Godden
kept in an English house a gorgeous blue Persian carpet like
the one that Sophie purchased in a moment of extravagance.[8]
One can only believe that Miss Godden bought her rug, as
Sophie instinctively bought hers, in the spirit of the Chinese
saying, "If I had but two loaves of bread, I would sell one
and buy white hyacinths to feed my soul."

Love and security, beauty and order, dignity and permanence—they are conventional ideals, even trite, but in an age
of anxiety and uncertainty when all values have come under
question from one quarter or another, it is refreshing and re-
assuring to find a serious artist seriously affirming their worth.
In a different way altogether, Rumer Godden reaffirmed these
values in her longest and most complex book, *In This House
of Brede*. This time the house itself, though important, is at
last put in its place as second to the characters. Indeed, in this
late novel the lives of the characters, intricately detailed though
they are, are secondary to the love of, and faith in, God, for
this "house" is not a family dwelling but a Benedictine
monastery.

II   In This House of Brede

If, on a map of East Sussex, a straight line were drawn between the nearby towns of Rye and Battle, the midpoint of that line would nearly coincide with the place called Brede. Few Americans who have passed Brede to visit the site of the Battle of Hastings would recognize the name of that South Coast village where Rumer Godden once lived for a few months, but it lies in a region that she knows well; she was born and schooled at nearby Eastbourne, and for the past ten years Sussex has again been her home after many years spent in India and elsewhere. In fact, she remarked after settling there that Little Douce Grove at Northiam, only four or five miles from Brede, was her first real home. In this region of marshes and woodlands she set the novel of her late maturity, *In This House of Brede* (1969). "Late maturity" is an advisedly chosen phrase, not because some of her early works were immature but because, unlike many novelists, she has continued to grow, to broaden her interests, to deepen her sympathies, and to increase the density of her books—even after writing for forty years—adding a subtlety of analysis to her customary richness of tint and surface design.

Predictably, therefore, the title of this late work is resonant with signification not only for the book itself but for a study of Rumer Godden as a novelist. The important word in this title is not "House," despite her long-held fascination with old houses and the families they have sheltered; the operative word at a number of levels is "Brede," for not only is it the name of a real place but it also has a long and varied history in the English language. The word *brede* has meant both bread and meat; and in the book the nuns are individually concerned with spiritual as well as material sustenance, the ordinary, rather tasteless diet prepared in their kitchens, the Communion Host, and the rarer nourishment that they seek through the elaborate liturgy and continuous meditation of their order. *Brede* has also meant "to weave, interweave" and "fabric" or "embroidery"—and here again it resounds in the mind; for not only do the nuns weave their own cloth, even fine silks, and not only is one of their regular occupations the making of gorgeous clerical vestments, but they are also engaged in weaving another kind of fabric: an endless bolt of praise to God, as their house is dedicated to doing in perpetuity. Still another resonance inheres in the phrase "House of Brede," for the nuns' medieval monastery is also a physical fabric; but it is now decaying and in need of renewing at many points, just as the lives of the nuns are constantly in need of shoring up, of inspection and repair.

Metaphorically, the book itself is a *brede* or tapestry; for the novelist has woven a seamless fabric of many different threads that are the lives of scores of persons: nuns, sisters, novices, and externs, not to mention the other lives which crossed theirs in the world outside Brede Abbey. That metaphorical tapestry is apt for *In This House of Brede* in more than the usual sense. *Black Narcissus* treated a house of nuns, but only a handful of them were individually realized; *In This House of Brede* characterizes at least twenty, names forty-five, and numbers ninety-nine nuns, and that is only within the enclosure and before the Japanese postulants arrive. While Philippa Talbot is the principal character, she is almost lost sight of in the densely detailed treatment of many others—two abbesses, several postulants, and four or five choir nuns, not to mention a few lay characters.

Miss Godden quoted Chaucer to the effect that "Life is a thinne subtil knittinge of thinges" in a prefatory note to *China Court: The Hours of a Country House.* As in *China Court*, the liturgical hours are the framework of the story of Brede, though much more subtly so; and, as in *China Court*, the life of an old house is temporarily suspended while its mistress lies dying. The careers of many persons are "subtly knitted" together, so subtly that not only is the author's intent not intrusive, it is scarcely evident until near the end of this longest of Rumer Godden novels. More than that, it is the most interesting, richest, most moving, and ultimately the most convincing of her books.

One reason for the excellence of *In This House of Brede* may be that, for the first time in Miss Godden's writing career, she is presenting a realistic story with intricately detailed representation of a highly specialized way of life—most particularly, a way of life that she has never lived herself. In other words, she did not begin *Brede* with a confident sense of complete mastery of her materials, as she had done with many other books; instead, she had to project herself imaginatively into the cloister, creating what she did not know directly. Of necessity, she synthesized the lives of the nuns from an outsider's observations of the liturgy and the daily routine, from long and intimate conversations with various Benedictine nuns, from the sounds she heard while living at the gates of an English monastery much like Brede Abbey and also while visiting a Frenchwoman whose poems she translated and who lived at that period in a French monastery, the Benedictine Abbey of Saint Louis du Temple at Limon-par-Igny. For the lives of the nuns before they entered, of course, she could rely on her own experience as a woman and as an observer of both men and women, just as any novelist would do and just as, before *In This House of Brede*, Miss Godden herself had always done. All her earlier realistic novels had reflected the particular experience of their author in particular settings.

Now, with *In This House of Brede*, she did something very different: she spent some five years in detailed study of the pattern of life in Benedictine monasteries, even living for a time at the gates of Stanbrook Abbey in Worcester. Although she immersed herself in the special routine she wished to depict, and although she probably identified herself with the nuns for years, nevertheless she has never *been* a nun. This outwardness contributed an artistic detachment that was new to her; and this detachment permitted her to avoid the occasional subjective provincialisms of earlier novels—the personal resentments, for example, that hang over *Black Narcissus, Breakfast with the Nikolides,* and *Kingfishers Catch Fire*.

That five-year period of study was not the only preparation she brought to her big novel. Although she had had a bitter experience with Anglican nuns as a schoolgirl, she continued to be fascinated by monasticism, and she once visited the Order of St. Bernard at Martigny in Switzerland to write an article, "Heroic Monks of St. Bernard." The Congregation, she wrote, is composed not of monks but of "Canons Regular, keeping the ancient rule of St. Augustine—love of God, love of one's neighbor, and the practice of charity." While the order is justly famed for its mountain rescue work, it "does not exist to train or breed dogs" but to train men.[9]

In exactly the same way, "this house of Brede" exists to train women—not to live in the world, but to live out of it, apart from the mainstream. Visitors there often exclaim, when they learn of the long hours of daily prayer, "But what do you find to say?" Answering that question is not the purpose of the novelist; but she indicates that steady application, continuous meditations, and rigorous discipline teach the nuns that, far from having too little to pray about, they have more than enough.

But why would a worldly and sophisticated woman, a respected government official, give up her life of excitement and power, give up the envy or admiration of others, give up the love and companionship of a man even more successful than she? We are never told; for Philippa Talbot does not share her spiritual struggles with underlings, and her conversations with her intellectual peers are reported but sketchily. One day at lunchtime she found herself entering Westminster Cathedral, whose spires were visible from her office windows; and unwittingly she joined the line of people waiting to enter the confessional. She was not even a Catholic, and later she wondered whether she had not been "led" into the church.

Why she did not retreat from this first encounter, how she was instructed and converted, and what were the motives which led her to take the veil—these questions are answered only by implication, if at all. Long after she has become a postulant at Brede Abbey, however, and even after she has been admitted to the full status of professed nun as Dame Philippa, she reveals some reasons why she *might* have felt lost outside—and why she may not even now be truly at home in "this house of Brede." Her husband was killed in World War II, and their small son died soon after in a terrible and freakish accident—he was buried alive in the cave-in of an abandoned mine. For some years afterward she had devoted herself wholly to her work; but it is the reader who must make the trite speculation that Philippa hid her pain and loss in work, for Rumer Godden does not tell him so.

And indeed Miss Godden could not do so, for her message is not of that superficial kind. When, two thirds of the way through the novel, Philippa is asked to become zelatrix, or mentor, to the new novices, she bluntly refuses. When the surprised Abbess asks why, Dame Philippa replies that she "can *not* be that" for Sister Polycarp, one of the novices. Sister Polycarp, it seems, is the daughter of the nursemaid whom Philippa still holds responsible for the death of her little boy. In her heart she has not yet forgiven that long-ago, unintentional, and no doubt exaggerated injury; she has prostrated her body before the altar, but her spirit is still uplifted in pride against her now dead enemy.

While a hasty reader may see this rejection of office as a minor plot complication, easily resolved, a more thoughtful one perceives that, for all the panoply and ceremony of Philippa's profession, habit, and daily observance, she is, nevertheless, hypocritical—a whited sepulchre; she is pure to the outward eye but full of sin within. She has found comfort for herself in the cloister, and she has even helped others with advice and prayer; but, in her conscience, she is still partly the servant of her selfish pride, and she still withholds part of herself. Until she can banish self absolutely, she will not be truly a bride of Christ. In short, although the novelist never obviously stresses the point, Philippa's refusal to yield is the key to the whole novel; indeed, it is the key to the way of life that novel depicts. In simple terms, the novel turns on the question of whether a brilliant and arrogant woman of the world can lose her assertive self and find happiness within the cloister. That question, however, is never expressed directly by the novelist or even indirectly by the characters. There is no preachiness, no false piety about *In This House of Brede*.

Moreover, Rumer Godden never evades either the physical or the spiritual implications of that rather vulgar question. For example, Philippa has been accustomed to liquor and tobacco; during her first weeks, she suffers genuine distress when she misses her brandy and cigarettes, even though they are not absolutely forbidden to a new postulant. Later, having mastered her body and having long since directed her mind toward steady contemplation, she is still uncertain whether her former habit of command will allow her *spirit* to yield—not to the Abbess's wish, not to her duty to her community, but yield to the will of God, which at first she can perceive only as a personal affront.

But Philippa is not stupid; she knows well what she must do, or renounce her commitment altogether, and to that end she asks permission to "take the discipline"—to lash herself—an extra time each week:

"If you must, you may," said the Abbess, "but only twice a week. Penance isn't meant to achieve a victory, Dame."

"Then what?"

"A surrender." The Abbess spoke with extreme gentleness.[10]

However, it is not the discipline that makes it possible for Dame Philippa to master herself by yielding; it is Sister Polycarp's gentle care when Philippa is very ill (ironically, with a disease brought into the community by Polycarp herself) that makes her foolish pride evident, though not in words, to the older, more sophisticated woman. Seeing not only the pride and the foolishness but also how petty they are when measured against the love and compassion of the younger woman, Philippa abandons them forever, and she enters at last without fanfare into the real community of souls. Recovering from illness, she is told to wash herself thoroughly and is given a new habit. "Feeling new from head to foot, she went to the Abbess's room and knocked."[11] In short, she has put away her old life and put on the whole armor of God.

This episode is the spiritual and intellectual climax of the novel. For readers who observe only incident, there are two or three plot climaxes, full of contrivance or coincidence, as Chapter 6 has pointed out. There are also eighty pages of story left, but the meaning of Philippa's retreat from the world is plain, and her surprising re-entry into it, clothed with righteousness, is an almost gratuitous demonstration of her success.

III *The Art and Craft of Rumer Godden*

Rumer Godden has a highly developed sense of drama. Indeed, the dramatic principle of conflict is so well understood in most of her stories that they can be and have been easily adapted for the stage and screen. At its simplest level in her novels and short stories, the principle of conflict finds expression in plain contrasts between physical conditions or emotional states, as between husband and wife or parent and child; in obvious differences between ethical or esthetic states, as between religious and layman, alien and native, sensitive and callous. At a second, more intricate level, she explores variations in these simple contrasts, as among the attitudes of westerners in India toward their Indian hosts or servants; or, as with *In This House of Brede,* the countless variations of attitude among the nuns toward one another as well as toward those outside.

No doubt Miss Godden was prepared for her role as delineator of human contrasts by the violent contradictions placed in her way almost from the day of her birth. An English child in India, she was protected in part from full knowledge of the rich life of that vast subcontinent, but by degrees as inevitable as imperceptible she came to understand, often without being told, not only that she and her kind were unalterably different from the Indians they dwelt among but also that the Indians differed from each other in a thousand ways, typified by the dozens of mutually unintelligible languages and dialect groups among them. Her own sense of alienation in England, when she and her sisters were sent "home" to school, can only have deepened her awareness that an individual, as well as a race, lives each in its own world, largely shut off from others. Time and again, even in the married state, her female protagonists are faced with the knowledge that no degree of intimacy can make two persons truly one.

Out of the immense complexity of human relationships it is necessary for the writer of fiction to select, to choose isolated instances wherein the truth of such relations can be analyzed in a manageable scale. Each writer, no matter how grand his vision or inexhaustible his energy, comes at last to the realization that he cannot write everything; and, because of this realization, he deliberately limits his scope. The extent of his landscape is not necessarily the measure of his skill or accomplishment; Thoreau traveled widely—and thought more widely still—in Concord, and Proust delved endlessly among the recesses of his own heart. It is therefore no diminution of Miss Godden's high achievement to say that many of her works turn upon the simplest contrasts.

Even when a Godden character is willing to learn and share in the daily life of others, however, insurmountable barriers remain between people—barriers not merely of language or mutual suspicion, but of inexperience and habit or custom. Sophie Barrington Ward, in *Kingfishers Catch Fire,* for instance, tries very hard to live like a native. Lacking funds to maintain the style of Europeans in India, she sets out to live among the inquisitive people of a small Kashmiri town. She takes a hillside farmhouse, acquires servants, cuts her ties with European acquaintances— and becomes a kind of hermit. For, although she is willing to become one of them, so far as she at first understands them, the people will not allow her to do so; indeed, they are unable to comprehend her purpose, much less her motive. An English-woman, she is therefore, in their eyes, very rich; the proof is that she can be cheated easily and does not haggle or seem to mind paying double. Even the crafty merchant "Profit David," with all his instinct for making money, makes the mistake of selling Sophie a beautiful rug she cannot pay for.

On her side, Sophie imagines that living among the people is the same as living with them; and, when she discovers their eagerness to buy certain herbal remedies, she is delighted to establish a herb garden and to prepare concoctions (regardless of the dangers of practicing medicine in ignorance) in the power of which she does not altogether believe. She is guilty of under-estimating Sultan, her steward; and, as a result, she is nearly killed by a love potion he administers in her food. Finally, she underestimates the herd children who drive out their flocks every day, and she scoffs at her daughter's fears: "But they are *children*. What could they do to you?"[12] Because she cannot imagine children's doing great harm, she forces her own children into situations in which they are nearly killed.

A comparable situation is presented in a *New Yorker* story, "The Oyster." Like Sophie in India, young Gopal in Paris finds that for all his desire to do as the Parisians do, there are barriers that cannot be leaped at once. Gopal, a Hindu, has never touched meat, fish, or even eggs. At home in Bengal his mother keeps an orthodox kitchen: "We shall not take life," she says.[13] In Europe as a student, however, Gopal has eaten flesh; and in Paris with his friend René Desmoulins he has even tried rare steak. In doing these things, he has been conscious of "what the world did to Gopal"—of himself on trial, as it were, in the customs of Europeans.

Now, however, he has met a new test, and for the first time he sees that, as a Hindu, he must be aware of "what he, Gopal, did to the world": "René had ordered the famous oysters and Gopal had looked so doubtfully at the plate of grey-brown shells and the strange, glutinous, greenish objects in each, that René had laughed. 'Pepper one, squeeze a little lemon in it, and let it slide down your throat,' said René . . . but, when Gopal squeezed the lemon juice on his oyster, he had seen the oyster shrink."[14] Even the rare steak had been dead flesh, already slain by someone else; but the oyster, shrinking from the lemon juice, is a living, sentient being. "Don't worry," says his friend, "it will die as soon as it touches you." And he laughs at the Hindu's revulsion. Gopal's indignation is towering: "You are a barbarian," he says to his friend:

"You all think we Indians should study your customs, why don't you study ours?" he cried to René. "We could teach you a thing or two! Why should we have to Westernize? Why don't you Eastern-ize? It would do you a lot of good, let me tell you that. You are cruel," cried Gopal. "You are not even honest. In England they teach children 'Little Lamb, who made thee?' and give them the roast lamb for lunch. . . . Yes! you eat lamb and little pigs and birds. You are cruel . . . and barbarous and greedy and . . . You are gross!"[15]

René, however, answers equably; he does not, in fact, even stop eating oysters until he has finished his dozen. And Gopal, swallowing his rage if not his oysters, is at last able to think with something like tolerance that neither East nor West is without its ugliness, its rank contradictions. Reflecting thus, young Gopal accepts his friend's grossness, and for the sake of learning and friendship he consents to try a dish of—chicken.

Contrast in regard to time and place is played down in *Take Three Tenses* and in *China Court;* for, after all, the theme of these similar novels is that both past and future exist in the present and that the history of an old house is a continual repetition of events. But contrasting settings in time and place are the very substance of *Chinese Puzzle*, Miss Godden's first book. The central figure of one section is a Chinese gentleman of the distant past; in the other part, it is a Pekingese dog in modern England. Similarities exist between the two, but similarity alone is not enough to bridge the gulf between them.

In regard to age and sex, contrast is a prime tool in most of Miss Godden's works, as earlier chapters have shown. Repeatedly she sets off a wife's subjugation against her husband's easy lordliness, and a child's helplessness against the "juggernaut power of adults."[16] In general, then, contrast is a characteristic device of Rumer Godden's fiction.

Another characteristic device achieves something analogous to certain effects of cinema or drama. This device may be termed a telescoping of dialogue with narrative or exposition, generally with the result that pace is increased and time sequences are scrambled. Watching a play on stage or screen, one experiences simultaneously the speech of the characters and an interior judgment or commentary upon both the characters and their speech. This partly unconscious commentary reflects upon the consequences of action being observed ("Ah, you've done it now"); it leaps ahead to anticipate action that appears imminent ("Don't open that door!"); and it pauses here and there to weigh the consequences of past action ("You should have thought of that when you. . . ."). The irony of this interior commentary contributes to the spectator's sense of the truth of what he sees by drawing him into the action as at least a minor participant, and by drawing him away from the theater and the seat he occupies.

The reader's involvement in fictional actions is produced by a similar irony, but he in reading a novel often experiences the double irony of analyzing the motives of characters who are analyzing their own motives at some former time—while both fictional times are being narrated simultaneously. This explanation looks complicated, but the real thing is simple enough (although it can be confusing) if the reader observes the shifts in person and tense that signal differences in fictional time. Here, for instance, is a passage from *The Battle of the Villa Fiorita*[17] (emphasis added):

Darrell and Fanny seemed of one accord, *we* were, yes, comfortable together, thought Fanny. . . . *she* had followed him unquestioningly, "Because *I* didn't know enough to question?" asked Fanny, yet now she saw that her happiest times had been since he . . . was away so much.

"Clavering shouldn't have left her alone," *they said* at the Club House.

"Damn it all, if a wife can't be faithful while a man does his work. . . ." *She could imagine* them saying that.

"But I was faithful, technically," Fanny *might have said*.

It is not clear to whom Fanny addresses her question in the first paragraph of that passage. To Rob after her separation from Darrell? To Darrell after the reconciliation which presumably follows the end of the story? To herself, perhaps—but no, quotation marks are not used regularly to indicate Fanny's thoughts. Certainly it makes no difference to the total effect of the story, but literal-minded readers may be put off by the device. Then, too, there is the awkwardness of getting such a device started, until the reader can take such shifts without surprise—as in the opening pages of *Battle* and *Kingfishers Catch Fire.*

Once started, however, the device functions fairly well in those novels. It permits not only flashbacks but "flashforwards," dozens of them, that illuminate the main action; and, through the deliberate irony of furnishing other viewpoints, it sometimes saves that action from sentimentality, or the language from cliché. That is to say, for example, that a trite situation can be looked at so wryly that the reader is beguiled into sharing the author's irony: " 'She never said a word,' and 'I thought we were friends.' That was Margot and Anthea, Fanny's best friends, 'Well, my oldest friends,' said Fanny."[18] Isn't it silly of them, Fanny seems to say, to confuse our routine familiarity with such intimate knowledge as Rob and I share? All but the most critical readers overlook the fact that Fanny can hardly have heard the remarks directly and that, besides, she is not retorting to any suggestion in them but presumably correcting herself in another context. And even the readers who do notice will be so bemused by the irony that they won't mind the underlying cliché: "Even her best friends didn't know."

Useful and effective though this device may have been, one could not help feeling, with earlier books, that it was sometimes lavished upon triteness, when it might have been employed to lift a fresh conception to positive brilliance. Fortunately, it has now been so employed in *In This House of Brede.* A single passage cannot possibly illustrate that claim, but a section from the Prologue to that novel may come as close as any. The protagonist, Philippa, is riding in a train from London to Brede, where she is to become a nun; and as she goes she is "remembering" not only past conversations with friends about her conversion but *future* conversations as well, events that she will not know until much later. This technique of near-omniscience resembles the "house voices" already noted in *Take Three Tenses;* it is as if, in addition to those voices from past and future, an omniscient third-person narrator had been fused with Philippa herself:

"Why suddenly?" Richard had asked bewildered [past conversation].

"It wasn't sudden, it was slow," Philippa had said . . . ten years ago . . . she had gone one lunchtime into Westminster Cathedral. . . . "I didn't know what I was doing there," Philippa told Dame Beatrice Sheridan, sacristan at Brede, to whom in her early days she often talked [future conversation]. . . .

"One of the good things about a Catholic church is that it isn't respectable," she had told Richard [back to past conversation]. . . .

"I expect I looked toward the line," Philippa told Dame Beatrice, "wondering what they were doing, because the old man beckoned me and gave me his place [future conversation again]."

"And disappeared?"

"I don't know," said Philippa . . . "the next thing I knew was that I was in the confessional" [ambiguous—to Dame Beatrice in the future, or to Richard in the past?].

"And did you confess?" asked Richard [past]. . . .

"Of course not. I couldn't. I didn't know how, but I asked the priest if I could come and see him."

"And that was the beginning?"

"Of the practical things. Of course I didn't realize then what I was in for."

"And when did you realize?" [ambiguous speaker—Richard in the past, or Dame Beatrice in the future?]

"I dodged," said Philippa. "Oh, I had plenty of excuse," she told Dame Beatrice [in the future, apparently answering a question different from the one preceding]. . . . the next step up in my department was a big step for a woman, but I think if I had waited a little longer I should have got it."

Richard confirmed that. "Indeed you would have got it [past]."

"For another thing," Philippa went on to Dame Beatrice [future], "I didn't want to be bothered. I thought I was very well as I was. . . . and all the while there was this strange pull. . . ."

"That's what happens," said Dame Beatrice.

"But *how* does it happen?" That was to be Mrs. Scallon's wail for her Elspeth, who was to become Sister Cecily [to Dame Ursula, not yet identified, in a second future conversation]. . . . *How* does it happen?"

"It happens in all sorts of ways," said Dame Ursula Crompton, to whom, as Cecily's novice mistress, it fell to see much of Mrs. Scallon. . . . It's as if God put out a finger and said 'You.'"

"I suppose it is the greatest love story in the world," Philippa had said [to McTurk in a second past conversation].

"Of course." McTurk had been his usual matter-of-fact self. "Like the merchant in the Bible who found the pearl of great price and gave all that he had to buy it."

"But I should have thought I was the last person," said Philippa.

"Why? You are a woman with plenty of acumen."

"But can I do it." In these last weeks Philippa had been more and more doubtful [ambiguous—is her doubt expressed to McTurk in the past, or to Dame Ursula in the future?].

"A vocation is a gift," said Dame Ursula [in a third future conversation]. "If it has been truly given to you, you will find the strength."

In the train Philippa began to feel she had no strength [in the present, without having heard Dame Ursula].[19]

This blending of past, present, and future actions goes down much more smoothly in the fabric of *In This House of Brede* than it does in this passage, lifted out of context and broken by explanation. Still, the passage ought to suggest the convincing immediacy and the sense of great richness in detail, of total immersion in the fictive experience, that this technique can achieve in the hands of Rumer Godden. Together with her happy interweaving of the various strands of narrative into the cycle of the liturgical year, this technique makes *In This House of Brede* a compelling and original novel. It is as startling in its own time as Virginia Woolf's *Mrs. Dalloway* was in its day. If Miss Godden has borrowed from Woolf and James Joyce and Marcel Proust, nevertheless two facts have to be acknowledged: first, that those are excellent models, and, second, that her style is as different from theirs as each of theirs is from the others.

It is, in short, an *original* style, and not alone because its techniques are unusual; another major reason is the perfection of its diction. One would be hard pressed to name another popular writer who has worked more carefully than Rumer Godden has to choose the right, the inevitable word in every situation in every story. Moreover, her passionate pursuit of clarity and precision has led her repeatedly into public declarations of her creed as a writer. Over and over, as in her articles "On Words" and "Words Make the Book," Miss Godden has insisted that mastery of diction is essential not only for poets but for all writers who hope to achieve lasting success: "If books were Persian carpets, to assess their value one would not look only at the outer side, the pattern and colourings, one would turn them over and examine the stitch, because it is the stitch that makes a carpet wear, gives it its life and bloom. The stitch of a book is its words."[20]

Not merely the meanings and the sounds of words but even their spelling, their appearance on the page, is of crucial importance to Miss Godden:

Another robber has been simplified spelling, though I expect no American will agree with this, but to me "color," for instance, has not the same weight and richness as "colour"; "center" is more diffuse than "centre" with its tightly coiled ending. A proof of what has been lost is that a great many writers will not understand what I mean by these differences; they will neither see nor hear them; and here, too, one has to indict the magazine "house style": an edited style to which all its writers must conform. Take the word "grey" or "gray." One magazine that I know will allow only the first, yet "gray" is not the same shade as "grey." . . .[21]

Because Rumer Godden with more than ordinary energy and persistence has sought precision in expression, and because she has brought to the search a poet's sensitivity to connotative as well as denotative meanings, she has been able to achieve an extraordinarily rich and suggestive prose—one all the richer for its subtlety, its simplicity, its apparent ease. So easy indeed is that hard-won precision, and so forceful entirely, that she can permit her reader now and then to share in the choice between two words, as when Grizel Dane meets her great-uncle in *Take Three Tenses*: "He put his hand under her chin . . . and his touch was not like an old man's. . . ; it was warm and vivifying. It surprised Grizel. What a blood he must have been, thought Grizel and clearly, like a bell ringing in her mind, she was corrected: *Not a blood. Not a blood, but a blade.* What a blade he must have been—and aloud she said softly 'Uncle Rollo!' and blushed."[22]

Having achieved, through a lifetime of writing practice, a

style both forceful and delicate, Rumer Godden is understandably intolerant of change wrought by others in the English language, even of the inevitable coinages that creep like byblows into the legitimate community of words. She has not been reticent about identifying the sources of pollution: "Jargon, too, has spread like a miasma over modern writing: technical jargon from psychiatry and science; pressurized jargon from advertisements; pep jargon from radio and TV commercials. You—Americans—invent turns of phrase that are original—and horribly memorable. They certainly put new vigour into English but they are boomerangs: They come back and hit the word that has been so invigorated that it often loses its intrinsic meaning and becomes a parody of itself. The true writer is continually having to rescue words."[23] Such is the influence of advertising on television and radio in this day of the transistor that not even the current printing explosion, let alone one author, can begin to hold back the tide of jargon. Language—all languages—continue to grow, as Otto Jespersen observed in the 1930's, through speech and not through the written word.[24]

Rumer Godden's prose style is made of many things, not only the contrasts both obvious and subtle which she finds in experience, but also the sensitive modulation among degrees of contrast; not only the diction both crude and delicate which she employs as narrator or gives to her characters, but also the fusion of two or more levels of language into an ordered and consistent whole. More is involved than these characteristics, however; and perhaps most important of all is her skillful poetic marshaling of images and symbols to extend the effects that she seeks to create beyond the mind and within the heart. Rarely are her figures obtrusive, drawing attention to themselves. As William York Tindall observed some years ago, "Whereas the 'black narcissus' of Rumer Godden's novel of that name seems no more than the perfume ignominiously used by an oriental dandy, it acquires connotations that justify the emphasis placed upon it. Sister Phillippa wants jonquils and daffodils for the convent garden. Like that perfume, these flowers of the narcissus family call to mind the original Narcissus, who, suggesting both Sister Clodagh's vanity and her rebirth, summarizes in one allusive image the principal theme of the novel. The blackness of this flower implies not only a nun's habit and the unworldliness that threatens rebirth but also the period of trial and deprivation that must precede it."[25]

It has been suggested in Chapter 4 that the symbols involved in *The River* are entirely natural and that they sink into the consciousness before a reader is aware of them as symbols. The river itself is one of the great streams of India, an immutable geographical feature; on its banks live Harriet's family, for whom the river is a hard fact that must be acknowledged in the daily movements of everyone. Beside it live other families as well, both Indian and European; and beside it, too, live hundreds of other beings, including the cobra that causes the chief crisis. But the river is also a figurative presence, not merely a literal one. Its unceasing flow, its perpetual flux in constancy, is perceived by characters and readers alike as a sort of whispered *memento mutare* that precedes and prefigures a bitter lesson Harriet learns: *memento mori*.

Still other frames of symbolic reference inform the story. Harriet's house is situated in a garden, not an extraordinary circumstance surely; but the Garden also suggests the innocence of Harriet and little Bogey who, partly because she fails to shield him, falls victim to the cobra. That snake, too, is symbolical—the Serpent in Eden, the type of Knowledge, of Evil, and of Death; and in Harriet's garden it is associated with the peepul tree—not only implying in the sound of its name the Fall of Man but also representing the Tree, in her case and Bogey's, of the Knowledge of Good and Evil. Bogey's name (though not the child himself) suggests in its similarity to "bogey-man" some Satanic influence like that in Paradise. Bogey's funeral procession, with flower-laden launches moving upstream on the River, marks the end of Harriet's childhood; it is their expulsion from Eden, and she longs to preserve both the happy past and the bitter Fall: "The river can't close over this, thought Harriet; then she seemed to see again, in the water, the handful of ashes that had been Ram Prasad's wife, and she remembered how they had been washed, round and round, gently, on the water, before the current took them away."[26]

Similarly, and quite as naturally as the words "narcissus," "river," and "brede" have occurred in other titles, the name of a bird has seemingly endless significance not only for the life of the main character of the book to which it is attached but also for the life of the author. "The real kingfishers lived down by the lake," runs the first sentence of Chapter 1 of *Kingfishers Catch Fire*. In Greek, "kingfisher" is Alcyone; in the old myth, Alcyone leaped into the sea after her husband died, and the gods in compassion changed the loving pair into kingfishers. Zeus forbade the winds to blow at the winter solstice, the time when kingfishers breed—hence the expression "halcyon days," a time of tranquility. Sophie, in the novel, leaped willfully into another kind of existence after her husband died and found in that existence an unexpected and temporary peace, her own halcyon days. The "Catch Fire" of the title probably alludes both to the G. M. Hopkins sonnet of being oneself from which the title comes and to the fact that a kingfisher is painted on Sophie's treasured lamp—and on Miss Godden's.

Chapter 3 of this study pointed out that a reference to caged birds was a way of emphasizing the predicament of wives mated to unsympathetic husbands, as in "Why Not Live Sweetly?" and *The Mousewife*. The plight of children at the mercy of adults is repeatedly paralleled in the condition of small animals and birds, trapped and helpless. And in *The Battle of the Villa Fiorita* both suggestions are conveyed in a remarkable passage contrasting caged finches with wild swallows nearby, much as Fanny Clavering has flown her humdrum marriage to live in "freedom" with her lover. A few pages later, to the rushing sound of swallows' wings, Fanny's children feel caught in a guilty act, touching the intimate things in her rooms and her lover's: "It was like putting one's hand into a nest and finding it still warm."[27]

This novel is interesting, too, in its use of suggestive names for persons in the story, a sort of nominal imagery. Charactonyms are not new, of course; Charles Dickens, W. M. Thackeray, and Henry James long ago found them a useful device, and the practice goes back at least as far as the medieval morality play. "Names are very important," says Val in *A Breath of Air*. "They are very indicative."[28] And his own name, as Chapter 6 pointed out, was the subject of some debate between Miss Godden and her American publishers.

In *Battle*, the unfaithful wife is named Fanny (Frances); the lover who steals her away from her family is called Rob (Robert); he is a writer, surnamed Quillet. All these are immediately, obviously, apt. Fanny is Mrs. Clavering, a name suggestive of "marriage" in its association with *cleave,* of "separation" with *cleaver,* and of "hesitancy" with *wavering,* all appropriate to her condition; and the fact that the name is not unfamiliar in England only makes its suggestiveness the more subtle and varied.[29] Her daughter Caddie carries the heaviest burdens in the story; she sells her beloved pony to buy tickets for herself and her brother in order to rejoin their mother, and she is betrayed by him before they have achieved their purpose.

It is amusing to notice, in connection with this novel, that the motion-picture version changed a number of names as well as situations. Fanny became Moira Clavering; Caddie, Debbie; and Rob Quillet, an English screenwriter, became Lorenzo, an Italian composer-pianist. About the film it may be enough to add that it starred Maureen O'Hara and Rossano Brazzi as Moira and Lorenzo.[30] Of course, American movie audiences could not be expected to take seriously a passionate embrace with Rossano Brazzi whispering "Fanny." In this case, Rumer Godden's was a symbolism of the *written,* not the spoken, word; whether trivial or weighty, it could scarcely bear translation to another medium. Only a very great artist of the cinema and a person of the highest esthetic integrity could be trusted to make the translation. A commercial moviemaker is likely to take only the situation and let the poetry go—a process which with Miss Godden's work is like keeping the rind and throwing the fruit away. Fortunately for *The River,* Jean Renoir, film director *par excellence* and son of the painter Auguste Renoir, undertook to translate that delicate fable from page to screen.

IV *Her Achievement*

Although Miss Godden's novels have gone through dozens of English-language editions and have been translated into a dozen other languages, and although she is a best-selling novelist in several countries, Rumer Godden has enjoyed an obscurity both with the public and with the critics that is hard to account for. One reason, of course, is that she has deliberately kept out of the public eye except under very formal and highly controlled conditions, such as, for example, in her lectures. Another parallel reason is that her private personality, like her public image, is quiet, controlled, and apparently placid; notoriety has never clung to her for a moment.

Still, her personal obscurity ought to make it easier to reach a clear estimate of her literary achievement, for that is not clouded by any very strong public impressions. Long ago, before her career had run half its course, James Hilton expressed the positive virtues of her work in this way: "Miss Rumer Godden's fiction had already won her a high reputation for sense and sensitivity; she has also shown herself a mistress of polished, filigree prose. In her new novel, 'A Candle for St. Jude,' she comes nearer than formerly to what might be termed a popular subject . . . but . . . her defense mechanism gets to work protecting the story from sentimentality and shaping it, indeed, into a rather subtle study of what it is and means to be an artist."[31] And later Virgilia Peterson gracefully deprecated the negative case: "If it can be objected that Miss Godden's reach never exceeds her grasp, it can also be argued that perfection, on any scale, does not need to be justified."[32]

Other critics have been both more and less admiring. The most attentive studies of Rumer Godden's fiction to date have been those of Orville Prescott and William York Tindall, both completed twenty years ago, halfway along Miss Godden's career. Mr. Prescott, in his book *In My Opinion* (1952), placed Miss Godden among the "select and superior company" who speak quietly about "the timeless truths of character and experience which are always the same, yesterday, today, and tomorrow":

A few writers can persuade their readers that they have cast a ray of light into the secret places of the heart, that they have increased by a mite the sum of human understanding about life and love and death, grief and loneliness and the misery of growing up. Theirs is no mean feat. It is a high art to distill the essence of experience into fiction. And to do so without adding to the general din, in a quiet voice, with taste, simplicity and sure technical craftsmanship, is to contribute something rare and fine to a world sadly in need of it.[33]

As is already evident, Mr. Prescott's survey is largely uncritical; but he does indicate that two novels, *Gypsy, Gypsy* and *A Breath of Air,* are not high accomplishments. He did not consider her two books published earlier in England, *Chinese Puzzle* and *The Lady and the Unicorn,* and his study naturally does not include her books published in the twenty years since his appeared. Nevertheless, his has been thus far the most sympathetic and comprehensive study of Rumer Godden.

Professor Tindall, for his part, placed Miss Godden in "the great symbolist movement of our time," along with Herman Melville, Charles Baudelaire, W. B. Yeats, James Joyce, Thomas Mann, Franz Kafka, and D. H. Lawrence:

Not all of Rumer Godden's novels are symbolist—or indeed poetic. Only the better ones are. . . . Fully aware of the tradition, she experimented with the technical discoveries and the themes of her immediate predecessors, Virginia Woolf, for example, and Katherine Mansfield. Among the Indian novels of Rumer Godden, two display the happy welding of thefts into new wholes of thought and feeling that T. S. Eliot commends. Of these, *Black Narcissus* (1938) is earlier and better; but, since *Breakfast with the Nikolides* (1941) is a first study for *The River,* let us take that next.[34]

However, "it is also plain that she is not as great as Joyce, Tolstoi, or Mark Twain."[35] For the allegedly general inferiority of her (then) later books to her earlier ones, Tindall suggested a cause: "Perhaps the requirements of a ladies' magazine, where most of them first appeared, compelled her to be incredibly obvious."

Depending upon others not only for method but for insight, she remains a craftsman.

Her forms, however, are uncommonly well adapted for communication. . . . she makes a vision clear to the common reader. Her function is translating the visions of major artists for those who could not receive them in the original. She does this by a surface so pleasing and limpid that it makes the depths immediately apparent. A fitting analogy for this effect is Sir John Denham's seventeenth-century river, at once the Thames and an ideal for public art:

> Though deep, yet clear; though gentle yet not dull;
> Strong without rage, without o'erflowing full.

Maybe her stream, like Denham's, is too clear. Great art is always mysterious; a great novel requires, invites, and rewards many read-

130   RUMER GODDEN

ings, yet we never get to the bottom of it. Although we can fathom
Rumer Godden at first reading or, in the case of that narcissus,
at second, the public novel, for which one reading is plenty, has
no greater master.[36]

For all his enthusiasm, then, Professor Tindall came to rest
in a rather condescending attitude. It is not too strong to say
that he betrayed a conviction that the truly great symbolists
are not intelligible to the greater part of the reading public,
and that any writer intelligible to them must necessarily be
somehow of lesser rank. Without debating the premises involved
in that implicit claim, one might well point out some exceptions
to the conclusion. Thousands of persons have read and appre-
ciated Melville's *Moby Dick* and Twain's *Huckleberry Finn*
without knowing or caring that the books are symbolical, and
one may also read and even love Yeats or Baudelaire without
much conscious awareness of their symbolism. (It is only fair
to add that Professor Tindall would not insist today upon all
the opinions he expressed in this article twenty years ago.)

Rumer Godden's mastery of diction, figurative expression, and
point of view, together with the universal sympathy and the
sense of harmony and order that pervade her works—all these
suggest in a rather fragmented way that she is a novelist of
maturity and power. Short of quoting a number of large seg-
ments from several novels, however, it would be difficult to
demonstrate very clearly the truth of that observation, for there
is no substitute for reading them in full. But, choosing a passage
to represent her "polished, filigree prose," we may take almost
any section from her best long work, *In This House of Brede;*
or from her best short work, *The River*—for instance, little
Bogey's funeral:

Father and Mr. Marshall came from the house carrying Bogey
in his coffin. They carried him down to the jetty and put him on
the deck of the *Cormorant,* and the people followed with flowers,
till there was a hill of flowers on the deck. Some of the flowerheads
fell off into the river, and were floated down and away. Then the
Cormorant cast off from the jetty and backed and turned in a half
circle to go upstream, and the other launches, with their people,
cast off too, and followed behind. Each launch left a pointed wake
in the water.

The river can't close over this, thought Harriet; then she seemed to see again, in the water, the handful of ashes that had been Ram Prasad's wife, and she remembered how they had been washed, round and round, gently, on the water, before the current took them away.

Now the launches had passed out of sight. The colours in the garden were deepening in late afternoon sunlight; it was nearly evening.[37]

Within the range of her subject matter and themes, few writers of English fiction in our century have approached the subtlety and power of her sensitive analysis of character under stress. As to plot and situation, she seemed less inventive prior to *In This House of Brede;* one felt that she would much rather work in a familiar setting among familiar kinds of people, and that she was lucky to have become familiar with settings and people that were exotic in Western eyes.

Every few years somebody hails the death of plot as a necessary element in the novel. Rumer Godden's earlier reputation might have benefited if that had been really true, for her plots sometimes seemed thin; but plot keeps coming back. The reason is that the reading public will not let plot die; they demand to be entertained, and they are not forever content to wait while an author probes yet another psyche. Now, with *In This House of Brede,* it is plain that a dense, complex plot is quite within Miss Godden's grasp and that she did not sacrifice subtlety of psychology or simple human interest to achieve it. One wondered, before this book, whether she might not be capable of producing a truly great novel, if she ever got hold of a grand theme in a powerful situation. The heart, the style, the technical mastery were all there, and her admiring readers hoped for still better things, better even than the splendid tale *The River,* better than *Black Narcissus* and *Breakfast with the Nikolides* and *Take Three Tenses,* strong and delightful though they were. With *In This House of Brede,* it seems clear, we are very near a novel of the first rank. On the other hand, one was forced to observe that in recent years her novels had appeared at longer intervals. Had she written herself out in the novel? It began to seem so, and then *Brede* dispelled the thought. After all, it is most unlikely that such a prolific writer should have nothing more to say, after forty years of finding more.

Millions of readers by now have warmed to the gentle wit and irony, the loving attention to animals and children and adolescents, the pure tones of English harmonized by a master arranger, and the delicate surprises Rumer Godden has found in the most familiar situations. To have delighted those millions in a dozen languages and a hundred nations around the world— what would any writer not give to have accomplished half as much? Rumer Godden's place in letters is already secure. If she is not yet among the most honored, she has long since been among the most loved.

Appendices

Genealogical Charts
of
the Families of Dane and Quin

APPENDIX A

The Dane Family in the novel *Take Three Tenses*

99 Wiltshire Place
1841–1940

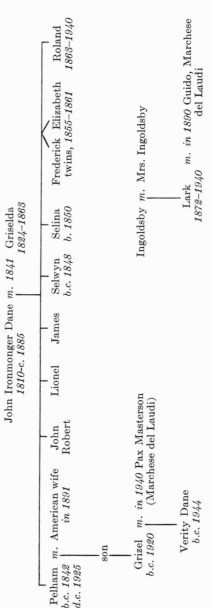

John Dane was called "The Eye."
Selina was called Lena.
Roland was called Roly as a child, Rollo as a young man,
and Rolls as General Sir Roland Ironmonger Dane.

APPENDIX B

The Quin Family in the novel
China Court
1840

135

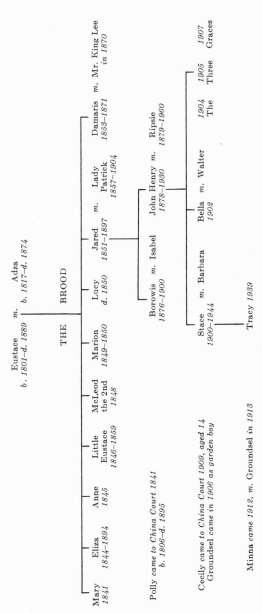

Eustace *m.* Adza
b. 1801–d. 1889   b. 1817–d. 1874

THE BROOD

Mary 1841 | Eliza 1844–1894 | Anne 1845 | Little Eustace 1846–1859 | McLeod the 2nd 1848 | Marion 1849–1850 | Lucy d. 1850 | Jared 1851–1897 *m.* Lady Patrick 1857–1904 | Damaris 1853–1871 *m.* Mr. King Lee *in 1870*

Borowis *m.* Isabel 1876–1900

John Henry *m.* Ripsie 1878–1930 1879–1960

Stace *m.* Barbara 1900–1944

Bella *m.* Walter 1902

Tracy 1939

The 1904 | Three 1905 | Graces 1907

Polly *came to China Court 1841* b. 1806–d. 1895

Cecily *came to China Court 1909, aged 14*
Groundsel *came in 1906 as garden boy*

Minna *came 1912, m. Groundsel in 1913*

Study of the Quin Family Tree from *China Court* by Rumer Godden. Copyright © 1960, 1961 by Rumer Godden. All rights reserved. Reprinted by permission of The Viking Press, Inc.

Notes and References

Chapter One

1. Jon and Rumer Godden, *Two Under the Indian Sun* (New York, 1966). So much of this chapter having been drawn from this autobiographical book, I have cited it but sparingly. Statements taken from other sources are, however, fully cited.

2. Rumer Godden, in a letter to me dated August 30, 1963, at Brede, Sussex.

3. Rumer Godden, in a letter to me dated April 17, 1964, at Rye, Sussex. Miss Godden once wrote that she went to India at the age of nine months, not six months; see her autobiographical sketch in *More Junior Authors*, ed. Muriel Fuller (New York, 1963), p. 101.

4. Miss Godden once called the professor her "great, great grandfather," not great-grandfather; see "On Words," *The Writer*, LXXXV (September, 1962), 17. This ancestor, Thomas Hewitt Key (1799–1875), was a Latin scholar, an author, and a Fellow of the Royal Society. At Cambridge, according to the *Dictionary of National Biography*, he was nineteenth wrangler (not eighth, as Jon and Rumer Godden say in *Two Under the Indian Sun*, p. 8). After leaving the university, Key studied medicine from 1821 to 1824 at the request of his father, Thomas Key, a London physician. In July, 1824, he met Francis W. Gilmer, an American who had been sent by Thomas Jefferson to seek professors, books, and equipment for the new University of Virginia; and Key accepted the professorship of pure mathematics. On the strength of his appointment, the new professor married Sarah Troward, youngest daughter of Richard Ironmonger Troward, on September 28 of that year and soon afterward sailed with his bride for America, taking up his duties at Charlottesville on April 1, 1825. He resigned in the autumn of 1828, officially because of the unsuitable climate but really, according to his great-granddaughters, because he refused to own slaves. For fourteen years he was

professor of Latin at the new University of London. From 1842 until his death in 1875, he was headmaster of the school attached to University College, London, and was also (without salary) professor of comparative grammar in the university. He was the author of many publications in philology.

5. Hezekiah Hingley's son George Benjamin succeeded (by special remainder) to the baronetcy on Sir Benjamin's death in 1905. The title became extinct August 19, 1918, when Sir George Benjamin Hingley died unmarried, as his uncle had done. See *Burke's Peerage* (1938).

6. "Down Under the Thames," *Ladies' Home Journal*, LXXI (April, 1954), 52, 203–6. This odd little story is indirectly explained as autobiographical by *Two Under the Indian Sun* (p. 59). In India, the girls had little commodes of their own (the "Thunderbox Club"); at their grandmother's London house, Jon and Rumer used a bathroom toilet seat with a frightful dark hole underneath: "'It goes right down the sewers to the Thames,' Jon had told Rumer, which frightened her so badly she could hardly ever perform naturally and had to be dosed . . . almost every night." Hence the situation and the title of the story "Down Under the Thames," published twelve years before *Two*.

7. "The Reluctant Lady Bountifuls," *Country Beautiful*, III (December, 1963), 16.

8. Jon Godden, quoted in a biographical sketch signed by Bernard Kalb, *Saturday Review*, XXXIX (July 21, 1956), 16. Jon Godden's novels include *In the Sun, A Winter's Tale, Mrs. Panopoulis, The Peacock, The City and the Wave,* and *The Seven Islands.*

9. According to *Burke's Peerage* (1938); see under "Hingley." Interviewed on the NBC-TV "Today" show, December 5, 1967, Miss Godden said, "My grandfather lost his wife and children in a very tragic accident. He was sent to the South of France to recover. He came back to England with a new wife, whose name was Harriet Rumer Moore, about whose background we never knew anything."

10. *Two Under the Indian Sun*, pp. 191, 193. See also her remarks about her religious training in "The Eternal Severities," *Vogue*, CXXVIII (August 15, 1956), 122.

11. Rumer Godden, quoted on the dust jacket of *Impunity Jane* (New York, 1965).

12. "Rumer Godden," *Book-of-the-Month Club News*, January, 1951, p. 7.

13. Rumer Godden, quoted in a biographical sketch by Richard Lemon, *Saturday Review*, XXVIII (December 3, 1955), 26.

14. Rumer Godden, in "Important Authors of the Fall, Speaking for Themselves," *New York Herald Tribune Book Review*, October

8, 1950, p. 5; also, as quoted in *Ladies' Home Journal* LXII (February, 1945), 3.

15. *Two Under the Indian Sun,* pp. 191, 193.

16. *Ibid.,* pp. 42–43.

17. The custom of Indians' bringing Christmas gifts (dalis or "dollies") to Europeans, described in *Two Under the Indian Sun* (pp. 118–24), had been given fuller treatment in an earlier autobiographical article by Rumer Godden, "The Reluctant Lady Bountifuls." The Hindu festival Diwali, also described by the Godden sisters, had likewise been treated at greater length by Rumer in "Diwali Lights," *House and Garden,* CI (May, 1952), 143, 198–99.

18. "Tightrope," *Ladies' Home Journal,* LXXI (October, 1953), 40–41, 94, 96, 99, 101.

19. Rumer Godden, in "Important Authors of the Fall," *loc. cit.*

20. "The Little Fishes," *The New Yorker,* XXX (Sept. 18, 1954), 78, 80–87. But in *Gone: A Thread of Stories* (New York, 1968), pp. 32–33, she explains that she and Jon never settled down at "St. Monica's" but were removed from the school by their mother after one year.

21. "The Little Fishes," p. 87.

22. B. A. B., "Authors & Editors," *Publisher's Weekly,* CXCVI (November 10, 1969), 18.

23. In *Two Under the Indian Sun,* pp. 207–9, Jon and Rumer say that Rumer borrowed fifteen pounds from her mother to pay for the publication of her booklet of verses; but see her sketch in *More Junior Authors, loc. cit.* There she says that she paid for the printing of her poems with her own savings, not with borrowed money.

24. Rumer Godden, in a letter to me dated April 17, 1964, at Rye, Sussex; also, J. K. Hutchens, "On an Author," *New York Herald Tribune Book Review,* December 18, 1949, p. 2.

25. Rumer Godden, quoted in *Ladies' Home Journal,* LXII (February, 1945), 3.

26. "Rumer Godden," in *Twentieth Century Authors,* ed. S. J. Kunitz and H. Haycraft (New York: Wilson, 1942). Also, *Book-of-the-Month Club News,* January, 1951, p. 7; Miss Godden's corrections to the Chronology printed in the front of this book; and *More Junior Authors, loc. cit.*

27. Hutchens, *loc. cit.*

28. Rumer Godden, in a letter to me dated August 30, 1963, at Brede, Sussex.

29. Rumer Godden, in a letter to me dated April 17, 1964, at Rye, Sussex.

30. *Ibid.*

31. Rumer Godden, in *More Junior Authors, loc. cit.*

32. *Book-of-the-Month Club News,* January, 1951, p. 7; also *Twentieth Century Authors.*

33. Rumer Godden, "I Wonder," unidentified clipping, dated August, 1956, given me by a correspondent.

34. *Thus Far and No Further* (Boston, 1946); the full title was *Rungli-Rungliot Means in Paharia, Thus Far and No Further.* The first English edition, published in 1944 by Davies, was titled *Rungli-Rungliot (Thus Far and No Further).* It was reissued as *Thus Far and No Further* by Macmillan in London in 1961. The dedication is "To Jon, and the spirit of little Joss, who was born there." (The reissue says *born here.*)

35. "About Rumer Godden . . . ," *Writer,* LXXV (September, 1962), 18; also the author's note at the end of *Kingfishers Catch Fire* (New York, 1953); and Rumer Godden, "Important Authors of the Fall," *loc. cit.*

36. Rumer Godden, "From the Author," dust jacket of the Reprint Society edition of *Kingfishers* (London, 1955). The novelist has explained (in a letter dated April 17, 1964, at Rye, Sussex) that the Macmillan edition (London, 1953) carried a correction to the name of the house in the Viking edition (New York, 1953): instead of Dhilkusha or Dilkusha, it should have been Dhilkush, meaning "heart's gladness." Note the similar name Dilkusha, of the Nawab Bahadur's country house in E. M. Forster's novel *A Passage to India* (1924).

37. Rumer Godden, in the letter just cited.

38. *Ibid.*

39. *Ibid.;* and *Who's Who,* issues of 1948–50 (see under "Foster, Margaret Rumer") and of 1951–63 (see under "Haynes Dixon, Margaret Rumer").

40. Annis Duff, "Rumer Godden," *Book-of-the-Month Club News,* September, 1963, p. 4.

41. In a letter from Rumer Godden to me dated August 30, 1963, at Brede, Sussex.

42. Jon (Godden) Oakley, "Rumer Godden" *Book-of-the-Month Club News,* May, 1953, p. 6.

43. Quoted on dust jacket of *Impunity Jane* (New York, 1954).

44. "The Poetry in Every Child," *Ladies' Home Journal,* LXXXII (November, 1965), 168.

45. *Ibid.*

46. *Round the Day, Round the Year,* and *The World Around,* "Poetry Programmes" published by Macmillan of London.

47. See *Book-of-the-Month Club News,* January, 1951, p. 7, and the accompanying portrait.

48. Jon Oakley, *loc. cit.*

49. Phyllis McGinley, "Rumer Godden," *Book-of-the-Month Club News*, February, 1961, pp. 5–6.

Chapter Two

1. *Chinese Puzzle* (London, 1936), pp. 2, 116–22, 148–49.
2. *Ibid.*, p. 5.
3. Rumer Godden, in a letter to me dated April 17, 1964, at Rye, Sussex: "I wrote this book [*Chinese Puzzle*] in longhand when . . . the capitalization seemed to me to give a good effect. Unfortunately, the book was taken in the same week that my first baby was born and I was not able to see the proofs."
4. *Chinese Puzzle*, p. 119. It may be noted that the cocker-critic's name is that of Bret Harte's white man outwitted at cards by a "heathen Chinee" in "Plain Language from Truthful James." Harte's James laments the dishonesty of the Chinese—meanwhile, revealing his own dishonesty. The dogs in Miss Godden's tale are not dishonest, of course; but the cocker James is baffled by the dark ways of the Chinese Ting-Ling, while Ting-Ling regards himself as sharing feelings and desires common to all dogs. Incidentally, the phrase "heathen Chinee" crops up in another book of Rumer Godden's: *China Court* (New York, 1961), p. 61.
5. Miss Godden has been a breeder of Pekingese; see *Thus Far and No Further* (Boston, 1946), pp. 119–20, 159; and *Who's Who, 1948–62*.
6. *The Lady and the Unicorn* (London, 1938), p. 61. This theme Miss Godden returns to again and again, especially as in this case when treating old houses; see, for examples, *China Court, Take Three Tenses*, and the story "Time Is a Stream." Note, too, that Robert's words are virtually a paraphrase of the opening lines of T. S. Eliot's *Burnt Norton*, first published in his *Collected Poems* (1936); later Miss Godden quoted another passage from Eliot's *Four Quartets* as an epigraph to *Take Three Tenses* (1945).
7. J. K. Hutchens, "On an Author," *New York Herald Tribune Book Review*, December 18, 1949, p. 2.
8. "Tightrope," *Ladies' Home Journal*, LXX (October, 1953), 40–41, 94, 96, 99, 101.
9. *Ibid.*, p. 101.
10. Joseph H. Friend, "India Declines Imported Piety," *Books*, July 9, 1939, p. 2.
11. See, for examples, Alexander Woolcott, quoted in "Turns with a Bookworm," *Books*, July 23, p. 14, as rejecting Friend's review; and Clifton Fadiman, review of *Black Narcissus*, in the *New Yorker*, XV (July 15, 1939), 59.
12. *Black Narcissus* (Boston, 1939), p. 185. Miss Godden is now

a Roman Catholic. Nuns, especially teaching or nursing sisters, are frequent characters in her work, though often incidental. One short story, "Sister Malone and the Obstinate Man" (*Harper's*, CXCI [July, 1945], 20–26; reprinted in Miss Godden's *Mooltiki and Other Stories and Poems of India*), has a protagonist who may be compared with those in *Black Narcissus*. Like them, Sister Malone belongs to an Anglican order, serves as a nurse in a hospital in India, and scarcely regards the natives as persons; certainly their religion is for her merely "Mumbo jumbo" (p. 26). Moreover, her faith by contrast with that of the "obstinate man" seems shallow or false; he at least puts his trust in God, not medicine. Later Miss Godden would "blush" to recall her treatment of nuns in *Black Narcissus*, and in her later stories and books the religious life and religious persons are handled with great respect. See B. A. B., "Authors & Editors," *loc. cit.*

13. *Black Narcissus*, p. 161.
14. *Ibid.*, p. 273.
15. Miss Godden has dramatized her own novel, but the screenplay was written by Michael Powell and Emeric Pressburger; it was produced (J. Arthur Rank; Universal-International) in 1947, with Deborah Kerr as Sister Clodagh, Jean Simmons as Kanchi, Sabu as Dilip, and David Farrar as Mr. Dean.

Rank inserted a preface explaining that these were Protestant nuns, but that avowal was not enough for some American Catholics. Three hundred nuns and priests, in a conference at the University of Notre Dame in July, 1947, protested that in its advance showings the film presented a community of "worldly, neurotic, and frustrated nuns" and therefore an abnormal case; and the National Legion of Decency condemned it as "an affront to religion and religious life."

Some American reviewers, thinking that attitude excessively severe, eagerly defended the picture; one of them claimed in the *New Republic* that "I found this a notably virtuous picture" ([September 15, 1947], p. 37). Others were more judicious. Hermine Rich Isaacs in *Theatre Arts* ([October, 1947], pp. 51–52) wrote that the film pretended to show strength in the nuns, "yet everything in the character and the actions of the group belies it. Instead of strength there is weakness; instead of dedication there is merely escape. . . ; instead of work there is a kind of hysterical inefficiency which, alone, would have been enough to doom the expedition to defeat." In this respect, it may be noted, the film was not unfaithful to Miss Godden's novel.

Chapter Three

1. *Gypsy, Gypsy* (Boston, 1940), p. 139.
2. *Breakfast with the Nikolides* (Boston, 1942), p. 247.

3. *Kingfishers Catch Fire*, p. 24. Notice that Denzil, Sophie's husband, works in "the little provincial town of Amorra in Bengal" (p. 7)—which is also the setting of *Breakfast*.

4. *Kingfishers*, p. 30.

5. The English editions of *Kingfishers* call the house Dilkhush, not Dhilkhusha. Each edition defines the name as "To make the heart glad." See note 36, Chapter 1.

6. *Kingfishers*, p. 7. In its details the story is sometimes autobiographical:

Dilkusha, the house in *Kingfishers Catch Fire*, is a real house, I lived in it for several years. I left it reluctantly some time ago, but it is still there on the mountains above the lake.

The book is not an autobiography, but I lived in Kashmir much as my heroine, Sophie, did. Like Sophie, I made a herb farm, worked in my garden, and taught my children.

The Kashmir that I describe was seen with my own eyes, watched and learnt through many seasons. (Rumer Godden, "From the Author," note on the dust jacket of the Reprint Society edition of *Kingfishers* [London, 1955].)

See also the nearly identical phrasing of a note by her sister, the novelist Jon Godden Oakley, "Rumer Godden," *Book-of-the-Month Club News*, May, 1953, p. 6.

7. The ingredients Sophie uses in her remedies may remind one of the similar list employed by a real Englishwoman in India who during World War II made and sold "Peter Pan Cosmetics" for the benefit of the East India Fund, as described by Rumer Godden in *Bengal Journey* (London, 1945), pp. 75–76.

8. Miss Godden once said (in a letter to me dated August 30, 1963) that "The Little Fishes" indeed "deals a little" with the school experience of herself and her sister. More recently, in *Gone: A Thread of Stories* (New York, 1968), pp. 31–34, she has made the identification much more specific.

9. Same letter; cf. *A Candle for St. Jude*.

10. *The Battle of the Villa Fiorita* (New York, 1963), pp. 49–50.

11. "Why Not Live Sweetly?," *Collier's*, CXIX (April 19, 1947), 11, 62–63.

12. Just as the captive dove in this Keats lyric becomes a symbol of the young wife's spiritual imprisonment in town, so another caged dove in Miss Godden's *The Mousewife* (New York, 1951) represents the "mousewife's" yearning for something beyond her drab mousehold. Keats's dove is offered peas to eat, but it dies; the mousewife's dove friend, also given peas, would have died too had she not brought him other food and eventually released him from his cage. Another

tie with English Romanticism here is that the story of *The Mousewife* was drawn from Dorothy Wordsworth's journal.

13. *Two Under the Indian Sun*, p. 196; see also 43, 116, 152–54.

14. "The Red Doe," *Collier's*, CXIX (May 31, 1947), 80, 83, 85. This story was reprinted, with a few modifications, in a section called "Himalayan Nomads" in *Mooltiki: Stories and Poems from India* (New York, 1957), pp. 68–81.

The deer-hunting incident, and its mystical union between hunter and hunted, may be compared with those in William Faulkner's "Delta Autumn," wherein an old hunter recalls shooting his first deer when he was a boy, and having his face ritually marked with the blood to signify a vow he was able to phrase only years later: *I slew you; my bearing must not shame your quitting life. My conduct . . . must become your death. . . . (Go Down, Moses* [New York, 1942], p. 351.) Note, too, that in both stories a slain doe is symbolic (like the caged doves) of woman as the victim of man's pride.

15. "The Red Doe," pp. 83, 85.

16. *Ibid.*, p. 85.

17. *Thus Far and No Further* (Boston, 1946), pp. 78–79.

18. "The Eternal Severities,'" *Vogue*, CXXVIII (August 15, 1956), 123.

19. "A Prince for All Seasons," *Ladies' Home Journal*, LXXXIII (March, 1966), 100, 188.

20. "The Most Unforgettable Character I've Met," *Reader's Digest*, LXVI (February, 1955), 118.

21. *Ibid.*, p. 120.

Chapter Four

1. *The River* (Boston, 1946), p. 136.

2. *Ibid.*, pp. 137, 153. The last line of Harriet's poem is suspended for some pages in this short novel, in a convincing imitation of real composition.

3. *Take Three Tenses: A Fugue in Time* (Boston, 1945), p. 3. Miss Godden has written (in a letter dated April 17, 1964, at Rye, Sussex) that the Dane house "was based on" her grandmother's London residence where the novelist visited and lived for a short time as a child.

4. *Take Three Tenses*, p. 7.

5. *Ibid.*, p. 164.

6. *Ibid.*, p. 165.

7. Cf. *ibid.*, p. 55 and p. 192.

8. *Ibid.*, pp. 56–57.

9. *Ibid.,* p. 12.

10. John R. Frey, "Past or Present Tense? A Note on the Technique of Narration," *Journal of English and Germanic Philology,* XLVI (April, 1947), 206–7.

11. *Ibid.,* p. 208.

12. Orville Prescott, in "Books of the Times," *The New York Times,* March 3, 1961, p. 25.

13. Miss Godden has been reported as saying that she wrote "nine drafts of *Take Three Tenses* . . . two of them as a play written only to sharpen up her writing style after her wartime years in the Women's Voluntary Service in India. . . ." (J. K. Hutchens, "On an Author," *New York Herald Tribune Book Review,* December 18, 1949, p. 2). It is surprising, in view of the care she took, that some striking inconsistencies should have escaped her attention; presumably she did not consult an American about the story, so Grizel is called "Lieutenant Dane of the U.S. ambulance corps" (*Take Three Tenses,* p. 73), and she is allowed such un-American idioms as "I shouldn't be [a discord]. . . . I should complete the chord" (p. 80) in a context in which an American would say "I wouldn't" and "I would."

14. "Time Is a Stream," *The New Yorker,* XXV (July 9, 1949), 19–23. Mrs. Throckmorton is reading from a book unfamiliar to her: *The Thoughts of Marcus Aurelius Antoninus.* "Time Is a Stream" has been reprinted with many small changes in *Gone: A Thread of Stories.*

15. *Ibid.,* p. 23.

16. *Gone: A Thread of Stories,* pp. 197–99.

17. I have provided a similar family tree for the Danes, and both are printed here as Appendices.

18. *China Court* (New York, 1961), p. 264.

19. *Thus Far and No Further,* p. 157.

20. *China Court,* p. 264.

21. *Ibid.,* p. 304.

22. *The River,* p. 6.

23. *Ibid.,* pp. 47–48.

24. *Ibid.,* p. 141.

25. *Ibid.,* p. 143.

Chapter Five

1. The phrase "abandoned child" is used by Jon and Rumer Godden in connection with the first of these events in their lives (*Two Under the Indian Sun,* p. 6).

2. "Down Under the Thames," p. 203.

3. *Ibid.*, p. 206.

4. "You Needed to Go Upstairs," *Harper's*, CLXXXIX (July, 1944), 170–72.

5. *Ibid.*, p. 170.

6. "The Little Fishes," p. 86.

7. "The Little Black Ram," *Mooltiki*, pp. 82–97.

8. *Ibid.*, p. 97.

9. *An Episode of Sparrows* (New York, 1955), pp. 211–12. Rumer Godden herself was indirectly involved in just such a theft of earth from a city garden; a caller in London said to her, "Did you know that your window boxes are filled with earth from our square?" (Rumer Godden, in a lecture with her husband James L. Haynes-Dixon, "This Strange Thing Called Talent," before the Woman's Club of Richmond, Virginia, December 4, 1967.)

10. *Ibid.*, p. 245.

11. Rumer Godden, "The Secret Garden Revisited," *New York Times Book Review*, May 14, 1961, part 2, p. 36.

12. *Ibid.*, quoting *The Secret Garden*, by Frances Hodgson Burnett, author of *Little Lord Fauntleroy*.

13. *The Greengage Summer* (New York, 1958).

14. *Breakfast with the Nikolides*, pp. 201–2.

15. *Ibid.*, p. 158.

16. *The Battle of the Villa Fiorita*, pp. 307–8.

17. *Ibid.*, p. 312.

18. *The Diddakoi* (New York, 1972).

19. *The Fairy Doll* (New York, 1956), p. 9.

20. Virgilia Peterson, "An Unforgettable French Summer in a New Novel," *New York Herald Tribune Book Review*, March 23, 1951, p. 1.

21. Rumer Godden, "Beatrix Potter," *Horn Book*, XLII (August, 1966), 392, 393.

Chapter Six

1. *Two Under the Indian Sun*, pp. 83, 84–86, 196–97.

2. *A Breath of Air* (New York, 1951), p. 10.

3. Miss Godden has said that her American publishers (Viking Press) "did not like the name Kenelm, thinking it affected, so we used Valentine" (letter to me dated April 17, 1964, at Rye, Sussex).

4. In the same letter Miss Godden explains McGinty's gross speech: "It is, I am afraid, the common parlance of most young airmen." After twenty years, McGinty's language seems mild.

5. *A Breath of Air*, p. 245.

6. "The Writer Must Become as a Child," *Writer*, LXVIII (July,

1955), 229. This article was reprinted from the *New York Times Book Review*.

7. "The Secret Garden Revisited," *loc. cit.*

8. *In Noah's Ark* (New York, 1949).

9. "Heroic Monks of St. Bernard," *Holiday*, XXII (December, 1957), 30, 32–37.

10. *Saint Jerome and the Lion* (New York: Viking Press, 1961).

11. In an article on "Beatrix Potter" in *Horn Book*, XLII (August, 1966), 392, 393. Milne, she said, could not be compared with Potter; for one thing, Milne did not illustrate his own tales, and "besides, for me, he always wrote with one eye on the grownups." That is to say, he was deliberately whimsical; and that was an error, because "small children, on the whole, are grave and like gravity."

Chapter Seven

1. Quoted in "Eternal Severities," p. 123. The passage from Aristotle is in the *Nicomachean Ethics*, I, vii, 16.

Some of the other ideas expressed in this paragraph were first suggested to me by Mr. Jean Renoir of Beverly Hills, who kindly sent me a typescript, *A propos de Rumer Godden*. Mr. Renoir was the director of the motion-picture version of *The River*, and he worked closely with Miss Godden in India over the making of that film.

2. *Take Three Tenses* (Boston, 1946), pp. 78–79.

3. *China Court* (New York, 1961), p. 45.

4. *Ibid.*, p. 47.

5. *Take Three Tenses*, pp. 148–49.

6. *The Battle of the Villa Fiorita* (New York, 1964), pp. 5–6.

7. Rumer Godden, in a letter to me dated August 30, 1963.

8. Jon Godden Oakley, *loc. cit.*

9. "Heroic Monks of St. Bernard," *Holiday*, XXII (December, 1957), 30, 32, 33.

10. *In This House of Brede*, p. 260.

11. *Ibid.*, p. 281.

12. *Kingfishers Catch Fire*, p. 151.

13. "The Oyster," *The New Yorker*, XXVI (January 27, 1951), 31. This story received many slight alterations for the collection *Mooltiki: Stories and Poems from India* (pp. 38–51).

14. "The Oyster," *Mooltiki*, p. 47.

15. *Ibid.*, pp. 48–49.

16. *The Battle of the Villa Fiorita*, p. 307.

17. *Battle*, p. 97. This device of style has drawn attention and, from unsympathetic readers, an occasional unintended tribute of parody:

It is a style, one finds straight off, that spreads even to the characters who "finish the author's sentences," suggests a voice, and "occasionally each other's," says another. "And tense-jump," a third might have added, "to express what they might have said."

Still it all seems somehow skimpy. Contrived, too, "made up," a ruder voice might have said. And there is no getting around . . . the fact that it is clever, a difficult piece of juggling, or the fact that it has little sharp strokes which rouse one, briefly, just when one has about given up on the whole shebang. What one is left with, really, is the queer sense of a fine intelligence at play—but not, one adds, "at work."

(Review of *The Battle of the Villa Fiorita, Newsweek*, September 30, 1963, pp. 88–89.)

18. *Battle*, p. 15.
19. *In This House of Brede*, pp. 16–18.
20. "On Words," *Writer*, LXXV (September, 1962), 17. Cf. the nearly identical passage in "Words Make the Book," *Ladies' Home Journal*, LXXXI (January–February, 1964), 32, 36.
21. "On Words," p. 18. The passage that follows these quoted words ("This is not fanciful thinking. Words were originally chosen to fit the things they describe. . . .") is repeated, like the preceding quotation, in "Words Make the Book," p. 36. One concludes that "Words Make the Book" (1964) brings into a single piece the thought and even the wording of two earlier articles, "On Words" (1962) and "An Imaginary Conversation" (1963).
It is worth remarking that Miss Godden has managed to get her preferred British spellings into the American editions of her books. Among those mentioned here, "colour" is found in all her novels, both those issued by Little, Brown, her first American publisher, and those by Viking Press, her second. Her complaint, therefore, is to be taken as against the "house style" of American magazines, not of book publishers; and the *Writer*, as my first quotation from "On Words" shows, also allowed "colourings."
22. *Take Three Tenses*, p. 80.
23. "On Words," p. 19.
24. Otto Jespersen, *Essentials of English Grammar* (University, Alabama, 1964), p. 17. A reissue of the 1933 book.
25. W. Y. Tindall, *The Literary Symbol* (Bloomington, Ind., [1955]), pp. 126–27.
26. *The River*, p. 131.
27. *The Battle of the Villa Fiorita*, pp. 4–5, 9.
28. *A Breath of Air*, p. 148.

29. *The Claverings* (1867) was a novel by Trollope: in it, Harry's brother is Sir *Hugh* Clavering (in *Battle,* Fanny's son is named *Hugh* Clavering). And then there was Sir *Francis* Clavering in Thackeray's *Pendennis* (1849–50), which may suggest *Fanny* Clavering. Clavering is also the name of a village in Essex.

30. *The Battle of the Villa Fiorita* (Warner Brothers, 1965) was written, produced, and directed by Delmar Daves.

31. James Hilton, "Rumer Godden Presents Romance on Tiptoe," review of *A Candle for St. Jude, New York Herald Tribune Weekly Book Review,* August 8, 1948, p. 3.

32. Virgilia Peterson, "An Unforgettable French Summer," review of *Greengage Summer, New York Herald Tribune Book Review,* March 23, 1958, p. 1.

33. Orville Prescott, *In My Opinion: An Inquiry Into the Contemporary Novel* (Indianapolis, 1952), p. 201.

34. W. Y. Tindall, "Rumer Godden, Public Symbolist," *English Journal,* XLI (March, 1952), 117.

35. *Ibid.,* p. 119.

36. *Ibid.,* pp. 120–21.

37. *The River,* p. 131.

Selected Bibliography

PRIMARY SOURCES

The first American edition is cited first in the case of each book except *Chinese Puzzle, The Lady and the Unicorn,* and *Bengal Journey,* which have not been published in this country. Following is the initial English edition, although some of the English editions were issued first. More than one hundred other English-language editions are omitted here, as are dozens of foreign-language editions; but American magazine publication is indicated.

1. Novels

The Battle of the Villa Fiorita. New York: Viking Press, 1963. London: Macmillan, 1963. Serial condensation in the *Saturday Evening Post,* CCXXXVI (October 5, 12, and 19, 1963).
Black Narcissus. Boston: Little, Brown, 1939. London: Peter Davies, 1939.
Breakfast with the Nikolides. Boston: Little, Brown, 1942. London: Peter Davies, 1942.
A Breath of Air. New York: Viking Press, 1951. London: Michael Joseph, 1950. Serial in the *Ladies' Home Journal,* LXVII (November and December, 1950); LXVIII (January, 1951).
A Candle for St. Jude. New York: Viking Press, 1948. London: Michael Joseph, 1948. Condensed version appeared in the *Ladies' Home Journal,* LXV (June, 1948).
China Court: The Hours of a Country House. New York: Viking Press, 1961. London: Macmillan, 1961. Serial in the *Ladies' Home Journal* LXXVII (December, 1960); LXXVIII (January, February, and March, 1961).
Chinese Puzzle. London: Peter Davies, 1936. Miss Godden's first book.

An Episode of Sparrows. New York: Viking Press, 1955. London: Macmillan, 1956.

A Fugue in Time. (See *Take Three Tenses.*)

The Greengage Summer. New York: Viking Press, 1958. London: Macmillan, 1958. Serial in *Ladies' Home Journal,* LXXV (January, February, and March, 1958).

Gypsy, Gypsy. Boston: Little, Brown, 1940. London: Peter Davies, 1940.

In This House of Brede. New York: Viking Press, 1969. London: Macmillan, 1969.

Kingfishers Catch Fire. New York: Viking Press, 1953. London: Macmillan, 1953.

The Lady and the Unicorn. London: Peter Davies, 1938.

The River. Boston: Little, Brown, 1946. London: Michael Joseph, 1946. Short novel.

Take Three Tenses: A Fugue in Time. Boston: Little, Brown, 1945. London: Michael Joseph, 1945; entitled *A Fugue in Time.* Condensed version called "A Fugue in Time" appeared in the *Ladies' Home Journal,* LXII (February, 1945).

2. Books for Children and Young People

Candy Floss. New York: Viking Press, 1960. London: Macmillan, 1960. Story, "Candy Floss," in the *Ladies' Home Journal,* LXXVI (July, 1959).

The Diddakoi. New York: Viking Press, 1972.

The Doll's House. New York: Viking Press, 1948. London: Michael Joseph, 1947. Miss Godden's first juvenile book.

The Fairy Doll. New York: Viking Press, 1956. London: Macmillan, 1956. Story, "The Fairy Doll," in the *Ladies' Home Journal,* LXXII (December, 1955).

Home Is the Sailor. New York: Viking Press, 1964. London: Macmillan, 1964. Novel for children.

Impunity Jane. New York: Viking Press, 1954. London: Macmillan, 1954.

The Kitchen Madonna. New York: Viking Press, 1967. Story, "The Kitchen Madonna," in the *Ladies' Home Journal,* LXXXIII (April, 1966), 39–46.

Little Plum. New York: Viking Press, 1963. London: Macmillan, 1963. Sequel to *Miss Happiness and Miss Flower.* "Condensed Novel" in the *Ladies' Home Journal,* LXXIX (December, 1962).

Miss Happiness and Miss Flower. New York: Viking Press, 1961. London: Macmillan, 1961. "Novella" published in the *Ladies' Home Journal,* LXXVII (November, 1960).

Mouse House. New York: Viking Press, 1957. London: Macmillan, 1958.
The Mousewife. New York: Viking Press, 1951. London: Macmillan, 1951.
The Old Woman Who Lived in a Vinegar Bottle. New York: Viking Press, 1971. London: Macmillan, 1971. "A Fairytale for the Whole Family," in *Ladies' Home Journal,* LXXXVII (December, 1970).
Operation Sippacik. New York: Viking Press, 1969. London: Macmillan, 1969. Story, "Operation Sippacik," in *Boys' Life,* LIX (Part I in March, 1969 and conclusion in April, 1969).
St. Jerome and the Lion. New York: Viking Press, 1961. London: Macmillan, 1961. Story in verse, "St. Jerome and the Lion," appeared in the *Ladies' Home Journal,* LXXVIII (December, 1961).
The Story of Holly and Ivy. New York: Viking Press, 1958. London: Macmillan, 1958. "The Story of Holly and Ivy" appeared in the *Ladies' Home Journal,* LXXIV (December, 1957).

3. Verse Translations

The Creatures' Choir. By Carmen Bernos de Gasztold. New York: Viking Press, 1965. London: Macmillan, 1965; entitled *The Beasts' Choir.*
Prayers from the Ark. By Carmen Bernos de Gasztold. New York: Viking Press, 1962. London: Macmillan, 1963.

4. Biography and Autobiography

Hans Christian Andersen. New York: Alfred A. Knopf, 1955. London: Hutchinson, 1955.
Rungli-Rungliot Means in Paharia, Thus Far and No Further. Boston: Little, Brown, 1946. London: Peter Davies, 1943; under the title *Rungli-Rungliot* [*Thus Far and No Further*]; a second English edition, by Macmillan in 1961, is called *Thus Far and No Further*). Reflective and autobiographical book covering several months in 1941 and 1942 when she and her daughters lived on a tea estate in the Himalayas, an oasis of peace in a war-torn world.
Two Under the Indian Sun (with Jon Godden). Published jointly in New York by Alfred A. Knopf, Inc., and The Viking Press Inc., 1966. London: Macmillan, 1966. The Indian childhood of Jon and Rumer Godden, novelists, with their two younger sisters.

5. Other Books

Bengal Journey: A Story of the Part Played by Women in the Province, 1939–1945. London: Longmans, Green, 1945. Wartime service history; printed in Calcutta.
Gone: A Thread of Stories. New York: Viking Press, 1968. London: Macmillan, 1968, entitled *Swans and Turtles.* Collection of twelve stories, nine of them previously published in magazines. The preface and introductory notes to the stories provide some autobiographical information as well as many revealing comments not only about these tales but about the author's methods in general.
In Noah's Ark. New York: Viking Press, 1949. London: Michael Joseph, 1949. Narrative poem.
A Letter to the World. By Emily Dickinson. Edited by Rumer Godden. London: Macmillan, 1969.
Mooltiki: Stories and Poems from India. New York: Viking Press, 1957. London: Macmillan, 1957, entitled *Mooltiki and Other Stories and Poems of India).* Collection of seven stories, five of them previously published in magazines, and twelve poems. The title story is really an autobiographical essay, extensively revised from the version published in the Winter, 1942, issue of the *Virginia Quarterly Review,* where it was entitled "Elephants and Orphans." Four other stories had appeared in *The New Yorker, Harper's Magazine, Collier's,* and *Life and Letters To-Day.*
Mrs. Manders' Cook Book. By Olga S. Manders. Edited by Rumer Godden. New York: Viking Press, 1968.
The Raphael Bible. New York: Viking Press, 1970. London: Macmillan, 1970.
Shiva's Pigeons: An Experience of India. Text by Rumer and Jon Godden. Photographs by Stella Snead. New York: Alfred A. Knopf and Viking Press, 1972.
Swans and Turtles. (See *Gone: A Thread of Stories.*)

6. Uncollected Stories and Verse

"Feast of Christmas." *Vogue,* CXXVI (December, 1955), 99–100, 102, 104.
"Handsome Young Bee, or What Did the Lotus Want?" *Mademoiselle,* LXIV (December, 1966), 94–95.
"The Sailor and the Seal." *Good Housekeeping,* CXXXIV (February, 1947), 44.
"Tightrope." *Ladies' Home Journal,* LXX (October, 1953), 40–41, 94, 96, 99, 101.

7. Articles

A. *Autobiographical*

"Godden, Rumer." *More Junior Authors*. Ed. Muriel Fuller. New York: H. W. Wilson, 1963, pp. 101–2.

"Important Authors of the Fall, Speaking for Themselves," *New York Herald Tribune Book Review*, October 8, 1950, p. 5.

"The Reluctant Lady Bountifuls." *Country Beautiful*, III (December, 1963), 14–17.

B. *On Writing and Writers*

"Beatrix Potter." *The Horn Book Magazine*, XLII (August, 1966), 391–98.

"Do Women Make Good Poets?" *Saturday Review*, XXXV (January 5, 1952), 7–8, 39.

"An Imaginary Correspondence." *The Horn Book Magazine*, XXXIX (August, 1963), 369–75. About Beatrix Potter and modern publishers' practice of "rewriting" for children.

"Last of the Great Fairytalers." *Saturday Review*, XXXVII (December 25, 1954), 6–8, 32. Reprinted in *The Saturday Review Gallery*. New York: Simon and Schuster, 1959, pp. 11–19. About Hans Christian Andersen.

"On Words." *Writer*, LXXV (September, 1962), 17–19.

"The Poetry in Every Child." *Ladies' Home Journal*, LXXXII (November, 1965), 168–70.

"The Secret Garden Revisited." *New York Times Book Review*, May 14, 1961, section 7, part II, p. 36.

"Words Make the Book." *Ladies' Home Journal*, LXXXI (January, 1964), 32; reprinted in *The Writer*, LXXVII (July, 1964), 14–17.

"The Writer Must Become as a Child." *The Writer*, LXVIII (July, 1955), 229. Reprinted from the *New York Times Book Review*.

C. *On Other Topics*

"Bread." *House and Garden*, CXXIII (April, 1963), 136–37, 230.

"A Cup of Tea." *House and Garden*, XCIII (March, 1948), 90–93, 178, 179.

"Diwali Lights." *House and Garden*, CI (May, 1952), 142–43, 198–99.

"The Eternal Severities." *Vogue*, CXXVIII (August 15, 1956), 122–23.

"Heroic Monks of St. Bernard." *Holiday*, XXII (December, 1957), 30, 32–37.

"The Most Unforgettable Character I've Met." *Reader's Digest*, LXVI (February, 1955), 116–20.

"The New Blaze of India." *Vogue,* CXLIV (December, 1964), 195, 277–80.
"A Prince for All Seasons." *Ladies' Home Journal,* LXXXIII (March, 1966), 100, 188. In praise of Prince Philip.

8. Letters to Hassell A. Simpson

May 2, 1963, letterhead of Little Douce Grove, Northiam, East Sussex (although as the letter explains that house had burned two weeks earlier).
June 11, 1963, dated at "Temporary Address:—Stubb Lodge, Brede, Sussex."
August 16, 1963, at Stubb Lodge.
August 30, 1963, at Stubb Lodge.
April 17, 1964, at South Ridge, Gun Garden, Rye, Sussex.
June 12, 1964, at South Ridge.
July 6, 1964, at South Ridge.
August 13, 1964, at South Ridge.
October 9, 1964, at South Ridge.
October 19, 1964, at South Ridge.
August 8, 1967, at Mermaid Street, Rye, East Sussex.

SECONDARY SOURCES

1. About Her Life (All items listed are brief sketches)

"About Rumer Godden. . . ," *Writer,* LXXV (September, 1962), 18.
B. A. B., "Authors & Editors," *Publisher's Weekly,* CXCVI (November 10, 1969), 17–20.
HUTCHENS, J. K. "On an Author." *New York Herald Tribune Book Review,* December 18, 1949, p. 2.
LEMON, RICHARD. Biographical sketch of Rumer Godden. *Saturday Review,* XXXVIII (December 3, 1955), 26.
McGINLEY, PHYLLIS. "Rumer Godden." *Book-of-the-Month Club News,* February, 1961, pp. 5–6.
OAKLEY, JON [Godden]. "Rumer Godden." *Book-of-the-Month Club News,* May, 1953, p. 6.
   Other information about her life is available in *Who's Who,* under "Foster, Margaret Rumer," 1948–50, and under "Haynes Dixon, Margaret Rumer," in editions since 1951. See also *Book-of-the-Month Club News,* January, 1951, p. 7; November, 1955, pp. 5–6; July, 1966, p. 7; and September, 1969, pp. 4–5. Less reliable are the entries in *Contemporary Authors,* Vols. 7–8, under "Godden, (Mar-

garet) Rumer," and in *Twentieth Century Authors* (1942) and its
First Supplement (1955), under "Godden, Rumer."

2. About Her Work

FREY, JOHN R. "Past or Present Tense?" A Note on the Technique
    of Narration; Based on *Take Three Tenses: A Fugue in Time.*
    Journal of English and Germanic Philology, XLVI (April, 1947),
    205–8. The critical acceptance of her unorthodox manipulation
    of tenses is "most significant."
PRESCOTT, ORVILLE. *In My Opinion: An Inquiry Into the Contem-
    porary Novel.* Indianapolis: Bobbs-Merrill, 1952. Chapter 13,
    "The Essence of Experience," deals in large part with the novels
    of Rumer Godden.
SMARIDGE, NORAH. *Famous British Women Novelists.* New York:
    Dodd, Mead, 1967. Contains a chapter on Rumer Godden, pp.
    109–16 ("Famous Biographies for Young People" series).
TINDALL, WILLIAM YORK. "Rumer Godden, Public Symbolist." *English
    Journal,* XLI (March, 1952), 115–21. Miss Godden belongs to
    the great symbolist movement of our time; although she is not
    so great as Joyce, Tolstoi, or Twain, "the public novel, for which
    one reading is plenty, has no greater master."

Index

Abbott, Lawrence, 61, 67
Alcyone, 126
Andersen, Hans Christian, 97, 101, 102
Anglicanism, 18, 24, 27, 38–39, 41, 42, 43, 48, 71, 85, 112, 141
Antoninus, Marcus Aurelius (*Thoughts*), 69 (n. 15), 144
Antony and Cleopatra (Shakespeare), 75
Aristotle, 58–59; *Nicomachean Ethics*, 59, 106, 146
Austen, Jane, 91

Bach, Johann Sebastian, 61
Baudelaire, Charles Pierre, 129, 130
Bengal, 15, 17, 28, 36, 46, 75
Bernos de Gasztold, Carmen, 25, 102
Bonnefoy, Robert, 73, 74
Book of Common Prayer, The, 62
Brazzi, Rossano, 127
Burnett, Frances Hodgson, 85, 102
"Burnt Norton" (T. S. Eliot), 62, 67, 140

Calcutta, 15, 26, 35, 36, 68, 98
Catholicism, 23, 25, 37, 42, 57–58, 71, 84, 94, 109–115, 141
Chaucer, Geoffrey, 111
Claverings, The (Trollope), 148
Corot, Jean-Baptiste Camille, 90
Creatures' Choir, The (C. B. de Gasztold), 102

Dalcroze, Jacques, 26
Dalloway, Mrs. (Virginia Woolf), 122
"Delta Autumn" (Faulkner), 143
Denham, Sir John, 129
deus ex machina, 19, 49, 90, 93–97
Dickens, Charles, 91, 126

"East Coker" (T. S. Eliot), 62
Eliot, Mr. T. S., 62, 129, 140
Euclid, 75 (ref. Millay, Edna St. Vincent)

Faulkner, William, 91, 143
Forster, Edward Morgan, 139
Foster, Laurence Sinclair, 26
Four Quartets (T. S. Eliot), 62, 140
Frey, John R., 64, 65, 144

Gilmer, Francis W., 136
Godden, Arthur Leigh, 15, 16, 17, 21, 26
Godden, Jon (Ruth), 15, 17, 18, 19, 20, 21, 22, 24, 25, 29, 31, 109
Godden, Katherine Norah Hingley, 16, 17, 18, 22
Godden, Margaret Rumer (b. 1907) birth, 15; early life in India, 17, 18, 20–23; early life in England, 18, 21, 24–25; unhappiness in England, 24–25; "plain appearance," 18; green eyes, 19; early development of literary talent, 19; early verses printed, 25–26; opens danc-

157

Godden, Margaret Rumer
  (*Continued*)
  ing school in India, 26; first marriage, 26; birth of daughters, 26;
  first novel published, 26; finding
  her own style, 27; difficulties in
  World War II, 27; later life in
  England, 28–31; second marriage,
  28; striking personal quality,
  30–31; writing for children, 30,
  89, 101–105; full, active life, 29;
  no settled home, 29, 109; her
  stylistic discipline, 31; concern
  with things more than people,
  29–30; abiding interest in poetry,
  30; determination to master her
  craft, 32; realistic view of experience, 41; emphasis on household
  and marriage, 44; theme of
  women without men, 44–52; in-
  completeness of women, 52–57;
  importance of wifely submission,
  57; importance of discipline and
  regulation, 57–60; concern with
  the flow of time, 61–79; emphasis
  on difficulties of personal relationships, 73; abandoned-child motif,
  80–91; sentiment, not sentimentality, 83, 91; artifice more than art,
  92–105; touching the heart, 105;
  sympathy with living creatures,
  106; affirmation of conventional
  ideals, 109; her most mature, best
  and richest writing, 110–111;
  sense of drama, 115; irony,
  119–120; technique of omniscient
  narrator, 121–22; original style
  and perfection of diction, 122–23;
  objection to simplified spelling,
  123; rescuing of words, 124; she
  does not attract notoriety, 128;
  "polished, filigree prose," 130;
  subtlety, power and sensitivity of
  analysis, 131; final mastery of
  plotting, 131; her secure place
  in literature, 132

Writings:

Battle of the Villa Fiorita, The,
  44, 52, 53–54, 80, 88–89, 98,
  99, 108, 119, 120, 126
Bengal Journey, 28, 142
Black Narcissus, 21, 25, 27, 35,
  38–42, 43, 68, 111, 112, 124,
  129, 131, 141
Breakfast with the Nikolides, 21,
  27, 44, 46–47, 54, 87–88, 90,
  112, 129, 131
Breath of Air, A, 93, 99–101, 126,
  128
Candle for St. Jude, A, 26, 44,
  51–52, 98, 99, 101, 128
China Court, 16, 25, 29, 59, 65,
  68–74, 90, 94, 96, 101, 106,
  107, 111, 118, 140
Chinese Puzzle, 26, 32–35, 38, 42,
  43, 92, 101, 118, 129
Diddakoi, The, 80, 89–90
Doll's House, The, 30, 107
"Down Under the Thames," 17,
  80, 81–82
Episode of Sparrows, An, 50, 80,
  83–86, 90, 97, 101
"Eternal Severities, The," 58
Gone: A Thread of Stories, 142
Greengage Summer, The, 22, 44,
  52–53, 59, 80, 86–87, 92, 95
Gypsy, Gypsy, 27, 44–45, 90, 92,
  98, 101, 128
Hans Christian Andersen, 28, 101
"Heroic Monks of St. Bernard,"
  25, 103, 112
Home is the Sailor, 107
Impunity Jane, 30
In Noah's Ark, 102–104
In This House of Brede, 25, 28,
  42, 55, 57–58, 59, 90, 94, 109–
  115, 116, 120, 122, 130, 131
Kingfishers Catch Fire, 19, 22,
  27, 29, 44, 47–50, 53, 59, 80,
  90, 91, 92, 95, 109, 112, 116,
  120, 126, 142
Lady and the Unicorn, The, 23,
  26, 27, 35–37, 38, 42, 43, 45–46,
  68, 74, 80, 91, 92, 94, 98, 99,
  101, 129

90259

"Little Black Ram, The," 80, 82–83, 90
"Little Fishes, The," 24, 25, 51, 80, 82, 103, 142
Mooltiki and Other Stories and Poems of India, 141, 143
"Most Unforgettable Character I've Met, The," 59
Mouse House, 107
Mousewife, The, 30, 126, 142–43
"No Virtuoso," 42
"On Words," 122
"Oyster, The," 117–18
"Prince for All Seasons, A," 58, 59
"Red Doe, The," 55–56
River, The, 19, 21, 22, 23, 29, 36, 61, 74–79, 80, 125, 127, 129, 130, 131
Rungli-Rungliot (Thus Far and No Further), 27, 29, 57, 73
St. Jerome and the Lion, 25, 30, 103
"Sister Malone and the Obstinate Man," 141
Take Three Tenses (A Fugue in Time), 28, 44, 50–51, 55, 56–57, 61–68, 69, 70, 72, 74, 80, 92, 96, 101, 106, 107, 118, 121–22, 123, 131, 140
Thus Far and No Further (Rungli-Rungliot), 27, 29, 57, 73
"Tightrope," 23, 36
"Time is a Stream," 42, 68–69, 140, 144
Two Under the Indian Sun, 15, 17, 19, 36
"Why Not Live Sweetly?," 54–55, 56, 126
"Words Make the Book," 123
"Writer Must Become as a Child, The," 101
"You Needed to Go Upstairs," 82
Godden, Nancy, 18, 20, 22
Godden, Rose, 18, 22
Greene, Graham, 93

"halcyon days," 20, 23, 126
Hansel and Gretel, 98
Harper's Magazine, 82
Harte, Bret, 140
Hastings, Battle of, 110
Haynes-Dixon, James L., 28, 29, 145
Hemingway, Ernest, 91
Hilton, James, 128
Himalayas, the, 20, 27, 38, 40, 43, 44
Hingley, Sir Benjamin, Bart., 16
Hingley, Sir George Benjamin, Bart., 137
Hingley, Harriet Rumer Moore, 17, 19
Hingley, Hezekiah, 137
Hingley, Isaac, 16
Hingley, Mary, 16–17, 21
Hingley, Noah, 16
Hingley, Samuel, 16
Hopkins, Gerard Manley, 50, 126
Hours (Bonnefoy), 73, 74
Huckleberry Finn (Mark Twain), 130
Huxley, Aldous, 61

"I had a dove," (Keats), 55, 142
In My Opinion (Orville Prescott), 128

James, Henry, 29, 126
Jefferson, Thomas, 136
Jespersen, Otto, 124
Joanna Godden (Sheila Kaye-Smith), 28
Joanna Godden Married (Sheila Kaye-Smith), 28
Joyce, James, 122, 129

Kafka, Franz, 129
Kashmir, 20, 27, 48, 117, 142
Kaye-Smith, Sheila, 28
Keats, John, 55, 104, 142
Key, Thomas Hewitt, 16

Lawrence, D. H., 129
Lind, Jenny, 101
Little Lord Fauntleroy, (F. H. Burnett), 102

Mann, Thomas, 129
Mansfield, Katherine, 129
McGinley, Phyllis, 31
Melville, Herman, 129, 130
Millay, Edna St. Vincent ("Euclid alone has looked on beauty bare"), 75
Milne, A. A., 104, 146
Moby Dick (Melville), 130
monasticism, 25, 37–42, 57–58, 94, 109–115, 141
morality play, the, 126
mysticism, 34–35, 40, 43

New Yorker, The (magazine), 24, 117

O'Hara, Maureen, 127

Passage to India, A (E. M. Forster), 139
"Peace" (Henry Vaughan), 104
Pendennis (Thackeray), 148
Petersen, Virgilia, 90, 128
Philip, Prince (Mountbatten), 59
"Plain Language from Truthful James" (Bret Harte), 140
plot, 42, 131
poetry, 30, 102–105, 123
Point Counter Point (Aldous Huxley), 61
Potter, Beatrix, 97, 146
Prayers from the Ark (C. B. de Gasztold), 102
Prescott, Orville, 65, 128–29
Proust, Marcel, 90–91, 116, 122

rabies, 21–22, 46
"realms of gold" (Keats), 104

reincarnation, 32–35, 42
Renoir, Auguste, 127
Renoir, Jean, 127, 146

St. Augustine, 112
Secret Garden, The (F. H. Burnett), 85–86, 102
Shakespeare, William, 99; *Antony and Cleopatra,* 75; *The Tempest,* 93, 99–101
spiritual power, 43, 115
"symbolism," 129–30

Tempest, The (Shakespeare), 93, 99
Thackeray, William Makepeace, 126, 148
Thoreau, Henry David, 116
Tindall, William York, 124–25, 128, 129–30
Tolstoi, Leo, 129
Trollope, Anthony, 148
Troward, Albany, 16
Troward, Richard Ironmonger, 16
Twain, Mark, 129–30

Vaughan, Henry, 104

Woolf, Virginia, 122, 129
Wordsworth, Dorothy, 143
World War I, 17, 18
World War II, 27, 64, 65–66, 69, 70, 113

Yeats, William Butler, 129, 130

Zeus, 126